Architecture U S A

IAN McCALLUM A.R.I.B.A.

ARCHITECTURE
USA

THE ARCHITECTURAL PRESS LONDON

The book was designed by the author and printed in Great Britain by The Shenval Press, London, Hertford and Harlow, on paper supplied by Spalding and Hodge Ltd., London; and bound by G. and J. Kitcat Ltd., London. Blocks for the illustrations made by The Engravers Guild Ltd., London.

First published 1959 in Great Britain by the Architectural Press, London, in Australia and New Zealand by Horwitz Publications Inc. Pty. Ltd., Sydney, and in the United States of America by the Reinhold Publishing Corporation, New York.

CONTENTS

ACKNOWLEDGEMENTS

I would first like to offer grateful thanks to the Department of Architecture, Yale University. Without the generous hospitality and recompense I received on the two occasions I went there in the capacity of Visiting Critic, the preparation of this book would have been impossible. Thanks next to the American architects who were approached with questionnaires and requests for photographs and drawings, and who, often working against the clock, responded with the utmost promptness, efficiency and goodwill every time; also to Mr David Gebhard for letting me see his unpublished paper on Louis Sullivan and George Grant Elmslie. Mr Cervin Robinson, official photographer of the *Architectural Review* in the USA, has, along with the other architectural photographers mentioned in the credits below, provided photographs of the high quality essential to a book on architecture.

I would also like to thank those members of the Reinhold Publishing Corporation, New York, whose constructive comments have, I hope, avoided those howlers that await an author from one country writing about another; they are not, however, to be blamed for any that may have crept in behind their backs.

On this side of the ocean, among my colleagues in the Architectural Press, I am particularly grateful to Mr Raymond Philp, Miss Maureen Franklin and Mr A. E. Doyle for help in the production of the book; to Dr S. Lang for her researches; to Dr Nikolaus Pevsner for his advice on the 'Background' chapter; to my secretary, Miss Angela Hill, for doing everything a good secretary should do and more, and to Mr Reyner Banham for all-round assistance and advice. It only remains to add that the responsibility for the selection of material and the opinions expressed in this book is my own.

Acknowledgement is due to the following for photographs: page 12: top, *The American Architect and Building News;* middle, Ian McCallum, Arphot; bottom, Chicago Architectural Photographing Co; page 13: top, *American Builder;* upper middle, E. C. Gardner's *Illustrated Homes 1875;* lower middle, Sheldon; page 14: top, Peter A. Juley & Son; bottom, J. R. Johnson; page 16: upper middle, W. E. Tatton Brown; lower middle, *Arts and Architecture;* bottom, Ian Nairn, Arphot; page 17: top and middle *Arts and Architecture;* bottom, Julius Shulman; page 18: top left, *Arts and Architecture;* bottom, Julius Shulman; page 20: top left, Ben Schnall; top right, David E. Scherman; bottom right, New York Public Library; page 21: top, Ezra Stoller; middle, Roy Flamm; bottom, Hedrich-Blessing; page 23: top, Michael Brawne; bottom left and right, W. E. Tatton Brown; page 24: J. Alex Langley; page 25: Louis B. Schlivek; page 26: top, Edward D. Mills; upper middle, J. Alex Langley; bottom, Todd Webb; page 27: left, Jay-Bee Studio; top right, *Progressive Architecture;* middle right, *Aluminium on the Skyline;* page 28: bottom, Lewis P. Watson; page 29: top, Universal Atlas Cement Co; upper middle, Louis Checkman; pages 33, 34: John Szarkowski; page 35: left, John Szarkowski; top right, Chicago Architectural Photographing Co; bottom right, John Szarkowski; page 36: top, John Szarkowski; bottom, Ian McCallum, Arphot; page 37: John Szarkowski; page 40: top, Fuermann; middle, Ian McCallum, Arphot; page 41: top left, Fuermann; right, Martin; page 42: bottom, P. E. Guerrero; page 43: top, P. E. Guerrero; page 44, *Milwaukee Journal;* page 46: top and middle, Ian McCallum, Arphot; page 47: top, P. E. Guerrero; page 48: middle, D. Pleydell Bouverie; page 50: top, Berko; page 52: Fello Atkinson; page 53: Ian McCallum, Arphot; page 54: top left and right, Hedrich-Blessing; bottom left and right, Ian McCallum, Arphot; page 55: top, W. E. Tatton Brown; middle, Ian McCallum, Arphot; page 56: top, W. E. Tatton Brown; bottom, Bill Engdahl, Hedrich-Blessing; page 57, bottom, Bill Engdahl, Hedrich-Blessing; pages 60, 61: Cervin Robinson, Arphotus; page 62, bottom left, Ian McCallum, Arphot; bottom centre and right, Julius Shulman; pages 63–70: Julius Shulman; page 71: middle, Roger Sturtevant; page 72, top, Roger Sturtevant; middle and bottom, Morley Baer; page 73: Ernest Braun; page 78:

bottom left and right, Ezra Stoller; page 79: Ezra Stoller; page 80: Julius Shulman; page 81: top, Arber-French & Co; page 82: Joseph Molitor; page 83: middle and bottom, John Ebstel; pages 92–94: Galwey, Arphot; page 96: top, Homer Page; bottom, Robert Damora; page 97: bottom, Ben Schnall; page 98: top, Ezra Stoller; bottom, Ben Schnall; page 99: top left and right, Ben Schnall; bottom left and right, Warren Reynolds Infinity Inc; page 101: top, Ben Schnall; bottom, Rufus Stillman; page 103: David J. Wager; page 104: middle, Ezra Stoller; page 105: right, top and middle, Gordon Sommers; bottom, Julius Shulman; page 106: top left, York Photographic Studios; bottom, Gordon Sommers; page 107: left, Morley Baer; right, W. E. Tatton Brown; page 108: top and middle, Shapiro; bottom, Hedrich-Blessing; page 109: top left and right, Hedrich-Blessing; bottom left, Joseph Molitor; bottom right, Frank Lotz Miller; page 110: Hedrich-Blessing; page 111: *Architectural Forum;* page 112: top left and bottom, Philip Welch; top right, *L'Architecture d'Aujour-d'hui;* page 113: bottom left, *L'Architecture d'Aujourd'hui;* pages 114, 115: *Architectural Design;* page 116: Arnold Newman; page 117: top, Gottscho-Schleisner; middle, Robert Damora; bottom, Ezra Stoller; pages 118, 119, 120: top, Ezra Stoller; page 120: middle and bottom, Reynolds; pages 121–123: Ezra Stoller; page 124: Louis Checkman; page 125, top left, Sam Lambert; bottom, Charles Eames; page 126–129: Charles Eames; pages 130–132: Julius Shulman, except bottom right, page 132, Ernest Braun; page 135: right, J. Alex Langley; page 136: top, Michael Brawne; bottom, *Architectural Forum;* page 137: top, Ian McCallum, Arphot; bottom, United States Information Service; page 138: top, Ian McCallum, Arphot; bottom, Ezra Stoller; page 139: top, Cervin Robinson, Arphotus; page 140: The Port of New York Authority; page 141: top left, *Vogue;* page 142: centre, Photographic, Detroit; page 143: Ezra Stoller; page 144: Photographic, Detroit; pages 145, 146: Ezra Stoller; page 148: Yale News Bureau; page 149: Robert D. Harvey Studio; page 151: middle and bottom, Trans-World Airlines; page 152: top, Walter Sheffer; page 153: bottom, Ezra Stoller; page 154: top left, Ezra Stoller; top centre, Ben Schnall; top right, Andre Kortész; middle, Ezra Stoller; bottom left, Eliot Noyes and Associates; page 155: top right, James H. Reed; rest, Julius Shulman; page 156: Julius Shulman; page 157: top, Deegan-Photo; bottom, Skelton Studios; page 158: bottom, Ezra Stoller; page 159: Richard Garrison; page 161: middle and bottom left, Robert D. Harvey Studio; bottom left, Bradford La Rive; bottom right, Ezra Stoller; page 166: bottom, Bill Hedrich, Hedrich-Blessing; page 167: bottom, Bill Hedrich, Hedrich-Blessing; page 168: Lens-Art Photo; page 170 bottom and page 171: Ezra Stoller; page 172: bottom, Fuller Research Foundation; page 175: top left, Walter R. Fleischer; middle and bottom, Paul Damora; page 176: middle right and left, Ezra Stoller; bottom, Ian McCallum, Arphot; page 177: Ezra Stoller; page 178: top, Robert D. Harvey Studio; page 180: top, *House and Home;* middle and bottom left, Julius Shulman; page 181: middle right, Dale Healy; page 182: middle, Hedrich-Blessing; page 184: Ben Schnall; page 185: middle, Hedrich-Blessing; page 186: top, Chicago Architectural Photographing Co; middle, Bill Engdahl, Hedrich-Blessing; page 187: top left, Hans Namuth; middle right and bottom, E. J. Cyr; page 188: top, Robert Stahman; page 189: top and middle, Ezra Stoller; page 191: top left, Cincinnati Art Museum; page 192: top, E. C. Valastro; middle and bottom, Ian McCallum, Arphot; page 193: left, Ezra Stoller; right, Ian McCallum, Arphot; page 194: middle, Louis R. Glessmann; page 196: top and middle, Ezra Stoller; bottom, Ralph Steiner; page 197: top, Fred Stone; page 199: top, Ezra Stoller; middle, Ernest Braun; page 200: top, Lionel Freedman; page 202: top, Fred Stone; page 204: top left, Eliott Erwitt; rest, Ezra Stoller; pages 205–207: Ezra Stoller; page 208: left, Larry Frost; right, Marvin Rand; page 209: Marvin Rand; page 212: middle, Julius Shulman. Photo of author on back cover: W. J. Toomey, Arphot.

PREFACE

This book has a single purpose: to present a cross-section of the best of American architecture today. It is not and cannot be complete, and the selection is a personal one.

The approach is biographical because, in architecture today, quality is in direct ratio to the calibre of the individual architect. We are not living in a time when the artisan-workman can make a contribution to architectural style; this responsibility, along with many others, rests squarely on the architect. He may bring in many types of specialist as collaborators and he certainly looks to the builder and workman for high standards of assembly and finish, but in the long run it is the quality of his imagination that gives us good or bad architecture.

With the architect and with no one else rests the praise or blame for that architecture which has no accepted name, but which is now the accepted architecture of the twentieth century: the great nineteenth-century engineers and theorists prophesied it and made it possible, but the architects have made it currency.

The new architecture stems from three main sources—Germany, France and the American Middle West. Among the men who have made it, there are four pioneers still living and practising, Walter Gropius, Mies van der Rohe, Frank Lloyd Wright and Le Corbusier, all but the last resident in the United States of America. In America, then, we can see working out within a highly industrialized society such as the new architecture always pre-supposed, ideas which sprang, not only from the American, but also from the European, forcing ground of the nineteenth century.

Our own mid-twentieth century moment still shows signs of transience—a new tradition in architecture is unlikely to mature in a mere half-century—but evidence of vitality and variety is plentiful, and nowhere more so than in the United States of America, where a prosperous and lively building industry, creative freedom and conspicuous expenditure—three conditions for great architecture—have come together in recent years in company with a property boom and a climate of opinion free from prejudice against the new, to produce buildings which are the first of our era to achieve wide popularity.

For the young European architect an American Grand Tour is becoming as important as the Italian was to the eighteenth-century English gentleman; apart from the buildings, he finds there a wider public interest in his subject than he is used to, an atmosphere of excitement that heralds something important taking place and, among the *cognoscenti,* a searching criticism which is an aspect of self-confidence.

Unfortunately, there are many who, for one reason or another, cannot visit America; even many of those who can find it hard, on a brief visit, to bring the architectural picture into focus.

That is the aim of this book—to bring the American architectural scene into clearer focus. The approach through personalities was chosen because, though architecture is partially an anonymous art and is in need of having expert attention paid to this aspect of it, its starting point has ever been, and ever will be, the individual creative impulse. A true understanding cannot be separated from an understanding of the men who made it, their background, their training, the vicissitudes of their careers, their heroes, their outlook and their inner convictions. No apology is made, therefore, for introducing American architecture in the form of biographies and, after a brief look into the past and the future, these follow in order of seniority, starting with Louis Sullivan, pioneer and frontiersman, who built the stockade, only to perish within it before the territory had been properly secured.

BACKGROUND

In common with all the great movements of history, the industrial, technical and social revolutions of the eighteenth, nineteenth and twentieth centuries in the process and among the confused consequences of which we are still living, have roots threading back to where it will take historians many a year yet to reach. The revolution in architecture is but one aspect of the upheaval, and the new American architecture but one aspect of that. Yet even here, and despite a great deal of scholarly research concerning its origins, much still remains concealed. In a brief introduction to the subject it is possible to do no more than outline the present state of knowledge and some of the conclusions it has given rise to.

It is not possible to trace the beginnings to any one date or person, but there are two men who stand out as representative of the changes which took place in nineteenth-century America—Horatio Greenough and Henry Hobson Richardson. The first, though practising as a sculptor for many years, is now recognized as a forceful apologist for the aesthetic arguments the new architecture finally made its own. Greenough's essays published around the middle of the century are the first reasoned criticism in America of the kind of architecture which forces 'the functions of every sort of building into one general form, adopting an outward shape for the sake of the eye or of association'; they are the first reasoned plea that architects should 'begin from the heart as nucleus, and work outwards'. His ideas, if not his style, have a striking contemporaneity for the mid-twentieth century architect. 'God's world', he said, 'has a distinct formula for every function and we shall seek in vain to borrow shapes; we must make the shapes,

Above, Ames-Pray building, Boston, Massachusetts, 1886, by H. H. Richardson; the Romanesque re-interpreted in a very personal way for an office building on an awkward downtown site.

Above, the railroad station, New London, Connecticut, 1885–87, by H. H. Richardson, shows a revived confidence in the handling of plain surface and an almost entire absence of historical allusion.

Above, Marshall Field Wholesale building, Chicago, Illinois, 1885–87, by H. H. Richardson; considered by many to be Richardson's masterpiece, the building was demolished in 1930.

and can only effect this by mastering the principles.' He urged architects to study the functional beauty of ships; 'I contend for Greek principles, not Greek things. . . . The men who have reduced locomotion to its simplest elements, in the trotting wagon and the yacht *America*, are nearer to Athens at this moment than they who would bend the Greek temple to every use.'

Greenough was writing at the height of the Greek revival, but with the close of the Civil War the monopoly of the neo-Classical gave way to a stylistic free-for-all ranging from 'Egyptian' prisons to 'Byzantine' cottages. It was a state of affairs that was to continue with the waxing and waning of different fashions for fully sixty years, during which a new architecture reflecting Greenough's precepts was to develop parallel with it, its own fortunes waxing and waning in reverse ratio to the taste for historicism. A developing building technology was to serve them both with complete impartiality, though where the architecture of passing fashion was to treat technology like a necessary but unloved servant, the new architecture made of it a partner, drawing from it lessons of principle such as Greenough had in mind.

In the interval between the recognition of the necessity for a return to first principles in architecture and the full development of the material and technical means which were to make of it 'something new under the sun', there developed the great talent of H. H. Richardson. Like all men of the kind who come at the end of one tradition but before the first flowering of a new one, historians have found it a difficult task to decide which tradition he really belongs in. Greenough forecast, in 1852, the place that Richardson, if unwittingly, was to hold during a career which ran from 1865 to 1886, when he said, 'The system of building we have hinted at cannot be formed in a day. It requires all the science of any country to ascertain and fix the proportions and arrangements of the members of a great building, to plant it safely on the soil, to defend it from the elements, to add the grace and poetry of ornament to its frame. Each of these requisites to a good building requires a special study and a lifetime. Whether we are destined soon to see so noble a fruit may be doubtful; but we can, at least, break the ground and throw in the seed.'

It was Richardson who broke the ground. As one might expect from his French Beaux Arts training he looked to the past for inspiration, but in a very different spirit and with very different results, from most of his contemporaries. In the Romanesque he found, as Sigfried Giedion has put it, 'forms which from the time of their inception have been bound up with the wall as a flat surface', and continues with reference to Richardson's near contemporary Berlage in Holland, 'The new aims derived from their study of Romanesque buildings, and not the fact that Berlage and Richardson used somewhat Romanesque shapes, are what matter.' Not only did Richardson reinterpret the plain surface, albeit in terms of solid masonry or stud and shingle, he was also able to express the clarity of his plans with force but without pretension in the elevations of his buildings; the combination of these skills and the impression they made, above all on Louis Sullivan, are what gives him his place in the history of the new architecture in America.

Quite apart from the influence of his solid masonry architecture, apart also from the fact that he was an early representative of a new type of professional man* with an office organization which, as Professor Hitchcock has shown us, was the type of the twentieth-century architect's office in embryo, Richardson must also be given credit for the important part he played in the development of what has come to be called the 'shingle style'.

Already by the eighteen forties the influence of English romanticism had begun to show itself in the wood-framed domestic architecture of America. Vincent Scully has named this the 'stick style' because of the 'emphasis given to structural and visual multiplication of the framing sticks'. It was largely a builder's architecture and by the 'seventies, with the rise of the professional architect, two new influences came to bear on it—historical precedent and contemporary foreign example. The first derived from a re-assessment of the Colonial heritage, an interest confirmed and broadened by the Philadelphia Exhibition of 1876, which marked one hundred years of American Independence. The second came from the pages of the English architects' and builders' magazines where the works of Norman Shaw were much in evidence, labelled (confusingly) Queen Anne, and exhibiting a new freedom in planning, with reception rooms opening widely about a living-hall. These, together with a flanking interest in Japan, gave birth to what has come to be known as the 'shingle style'.

The 'shingle style' represents three notable innovations in American domestic architecture, open planning (particularly of the ground floor), a new sense of spatial relationships, both between one interior space and another, and between these and the exterior (making use of porches, called piazzas, as a medium of transition), and the professional and consciously 'aesthetic' use of a light wooden sheath for the exterior walls. The last, which is the most immediately recognized characteristic of the style and which gave it its name, derives in part from the light nailed wood frame (an American invention of the early nineteenth century made practicable by the manufacture of machine-made nails), sheathed, as an essential part of its structural stability, with boarding. This 'wrap-around' principle, in complete contrast to the exposed framing of the 'stick style', was exploited by the architects of the 'shingle style' sometimes to extravagantly picturesque ends, with cedar tiles undulating and bulging in curves of complex plasticity.

It seems that along the Atlantic seaboard in the decade between the late 'seventies and 'eighties there was struggling to emerge a new kind of domestic architecture, uninvolved with the superficialities of past styles, an architecture closely related to the lives and outlook of the people who inhabited it. These shingle-clad houses designed by men such as William Ralph Emerson, McKim, Mead and White, Bruce Price and H. H. Richardson, achieved a range of expression perfectly able to encompass the simplest gardener's cottage as well as mansions which, if lacking ostentation, were luxurious enough, one would have thought, for most millionaires.

* The mid-nineteenth century in America marked the end of the era of the master builder and the amateur architect. The Civil Engineers formed themselves into a society in 1852; the American Institute of Architects was founded in 1857, and the first architectural school in America—the Massachusetts Institute of Technology—in 1866. The first architectural journal appeared in Philadelphia in 1868.

Above, one of the buildings which comprised the British exhibit in the 1876 Philadelphia Centennial Exhibition; in the manner of Norman Shaw, they were the work of Thomas Harris and their style was labelled 'Queen Anne'.

Above, design for a 'Planter's House', 1875, by E. C. Gardner; the wooden framing is expressed in the characteristic manner of the 'stick style'; the roof and porch clearly show the contributing influence of Japan.

Above, Stoughton house, Cambridge, Massachusetts, 1882–83, by H. H. Richardson; a pure and restrained example of the mature shingle style.

Above, Cyrus McCormick house, Richfield Springs, New York, 1880–81, by McKim, Mead and White; a design which makes the fullest use of porches (or piazzas) to link interior and exterior space and in the detail of which Stanford White's skill in exploiting Japanese incident is particularly marked.

*Left, Brooklyn Bridge,
New York City, by
John A. Roebling; completed
in 1883, this is a perspective
made from Roebling's plans
before the bridge was built.*

*Below, Mercantile Exchange
building, 1882, by H. J.
Schwarzmann; a façade
constructed entirely of cast
iron, but taking its form and
ornamentation directly from
masonry practice.*

But, for complex reasons, among them the growth of the large architectural practice, the prestige of a Beaux Art training and the amassing of, for America, some unprecedentedly large fortunes, a reaction set in against native simplicity and originality, in favour of a stricter attention to historical precedent and an aping of European 'princely' manners. Much fine work was to be undertaken in the east during the next forty years, but except for buildings considered suitable for utilitarian treatment like the concourse of Pennsylvania Station, or superb works of engineering like Roebling's Brooklyn Bridge, little of it is relevant to the story of the new architecture.

Instead, attention shifts to Chicago where the independence and aggressive self-reliance of the middle west, coupled with a building boom which followed the fire of 1871, was providing architects with some spectacular opportunities, not only in the domestic, but also in the commercial field. Here, between 1885 and 1900, was developed a new type of building—the steel-frame 'skyscraper' office block. In 1885 H. H. Richardson had completed a wholesale warehouse for Marshall Field's, a monumentally simple and massive masonry block. Though the Field warehouse contributed little to the drama of structural innovation about to be played, and though William Le Baron Jenny's Home Insurance building (the first steel-frame structure, underway at the same time as the Field warehouse) contributed little to the drama of the struggle for 'psychological expressiveness' in the vertical office block, taken together they are clearly the founding buildings of the Chicago school.

What gives the Field warehouse its special importance is its influence on Louis Sullivan not only in the Auditorium building (the great opera house-office block he and Adler built in Chicago in 1887–89), so clearly following Richardson's example in structure as well as in the handling of its plain masonry surfaces, but also, though less obviously, in steel-frame skyscrapers like the Wainwright and Guaranty buildings, where Sullivan was concerned to achieve a significant expression for the tall frame building. It can be argued that he was ahead of his time and place in this endeavour, even that the model he took was an inappropriate one to the problem in hand. Monumental and impressively fine as they are, these self-consciously 'designed' skyscrapers now seem slightly outside the direct line of development of the new architecture, whereas the Chicago buildings of the practical men, the architects who were less concerned with expression, and more with the speedy and efficient erection of frame buildings for commercial purposes, have an almost uncanny nearness across the years. Did Sullivan finally realize this himself? For, in his last major building—the Carson, Pirie, Scott Store—he was to build the finest monument of the Chicago School, using the elements by which it is most clearly recognized —the wide, triple 'Chicago' windows, and around them the unadorned and unemphasized verticals and horizontals of columns and beams—with a finesse and self-confidence that makes the building a fitting swan-song to the great man's effective years.

It was around 1893, with the phenomenally successful Chicago World Fair, that the eclectic standards in architecture which the east had nailed to its masthead a little earlier, were carried to Chicago and established them-

Above, Pennsylvania Station, New York, 1906–10, by McKim, Mead and White.

Above, Guaranty building, Buffalo, New York, 1893, by Louis Sullivan. Below, Reliance building, Chicago, Illinois, 1894, by Daniel Burnham.

Above, Gale house, Oak Park, Illinois, 1909, by Frank Lloyd Wright.

Above, Hallidie building, San Francisco, California, 1918, by Willis Polk, an early example of the all-glass façade without parallel in California during the first half of the twentieth century.

Above, Blacker house, Pasadena, California, 1907, by Greene and Greene; one of the founding buildings of what has come to be known as the Bay Region style.

Above, Rotunda, Palace of the Fine Arts, San Francisco, California, 1915, by Bernard Maybeck; an exhibition building made of cement on a metal armature.

selves for much the same reasons as in the east and, but for skirmishes in the suburbs, against all opposition. Had it not been for Sullivan's pupil Frank Lloyd Wright, who, with a small band of like-thinking men, among them George Elmslie, Hugh Garden, George Maher and Walter Burley Griffin, kept the cause alive in the domestic architecture of the Chicago suburb, the mid-west would have warranted very little space in architectural histories during the next half-century.

In the years after 1900 Frank Lloyd Wright stands out as a giant. His houses carried on the development started by the architects of the shingle style, though before long they gave evidence of a creative artist ready and able to say something new and to say it in a regional idiom that was in no narrow sense provincial. Wright's Midway Gardens of 1914 showed what he was capable of had he been allowed to design buildings for leisure on a scale within the range of his talents. His unrealized commercial projects, particularly those of the 'twenties, showed what Chicago's loss of artistic faith in itself, lost it in the architecture of commerce which had been its proudest boast.

As, around the turn of the century, Chicago's creative vitality declined, so California entered the picture. In the San Francisco Bay region, the brothers Greene were building houses which were a Californian development of the earlier 'stick style' of the eastern states, but their open plans and the relationship they established between indoors and out bring them nearer to the mature 'shingle' than to the 'stick style'; in common with the architecture of the Atlantic seaboard there is a contributing oriental influence and a more marked one, as might be expected on the Pacific coast. 'The positive quality which emerges', says Vincent Scully, 'is that of the skeletal pavilion', and it is this quality which recurs in the Californian architecture of our own day by such men as Harwell Hamilton Harris, William Wilson Wurster and Joseph Escherick.

Bernard Maybeck, the University of California's first instructor in architecture and another outstanding figure of Californian regionalism (he died in 1956 at the age of 94), was both considerably more of an eclectic (see his Palace of the Fine Arts 1915) and considerably more of an innovator than the brothers Greene. In his Church of Christ Scientist, Berkeley, 1910, the oriental flavour is more than a discreet allusion, but side by side with it are standard factory windows and asbestos sheets, completely assimilated to make a masterly and very individual building.

Perhaps more remarkable to the European eye are the works of Irving Gill and R. M. Schindler. Gill, who worked for Sullivan in Chicago, came to San Diego in 1893. Showing, at first, the influence of Sullivan, he was soon to develop a distinct style of his own, employing, in his own words, 'the straight line, the arch, the cube and the circle—the mightiest of lines'. These buildings of poured concrete, of which the first was constructed in 1907, have a strong affinity with the buildings of the early modern movement in Europe, though Gill's inspiration is said to derive from a very different source—California's Spanish missions.

Schindler went to Chicago from Vienna at the age of twenty-three in 1913 and joined Frank Lloyd Wright's office in 1916 to work on the Imperial Hotel, Tokyo. He stayed with Wright for four years and then moved

*Right, Eingham house,
Montecito, California, 1917,
by Bernard Maybeck;
looking from the pergola
towards the living-room wing.*

*Right, First Church of Christ
Scientist, Berkeley, California,
1910, by Bernard Maybeck;
a mixture of gothic and
oriental motifs with asbestos
sheets and factory windows.*

*Right, Dodge house,
Los Angeles, California, 1916,
by Irving Gill, a structure of
poured concrete with forms
deriving from the architecture
of the California missions.*

Above left, Lovell house, Newport beach, California, 1926, by
R. M. Schindler; in order to raise the living area above the public
beach the house is hung from concrete pylons.
Above right, Freeman house, Los Angeles, California, 1924, by

Frank Lloyd Wright; one of the 'textile-block' houses.
Below, Lovell house, Los Angeles, California, 1927, by Richard
Neutra; a meeting point between the modern movement in Europe,
the American Middle West, and California.

to California to supervise the construction of Wright's Barnsdall house. There he stayed, setting up in practice on his own and building a house and office for himself in 1921. The way in which he employed skeleton structures of exposed concrete with overlapping horizontal ribbons and counterbalancing verticals, the manner of interplay of solids and voids, are often reminiscent of the Dutch de Stijl group, and his work would seem to be nearer in spirit to Europe than any other being done in America at that time.

The Californian houses of Frank Lloyd Wright are a very different thing; an outcrop by an individual genius applying his talents to a method of construction—'the Textile Block'—and a region foreign to himself in climate and vegetation to produce what proved to be isolated works. Contemporary critics would have been justified in considering them a promising beginning for a new and specifically Californian architecture but, yet again, the effects of an exhibition were spreading a taste for period imitation and stultifying the development of the new architecture.

Just as the Philadelphia Centennial of 1873 finally led to a hardening of hearts against native originality in architecture by displaying the more sophisticated and highly developed styles of the Colonial and 'Queen Anne'; just as the Chicago World Fair of 1893 offered what proved to be the irresistible attractions of Beaux Arts neo-Baroque, so the San Diego Fair of 1915 encouraged a return to Spanish Colonial in California. Soon the Greenes found it necessary to close their office for lack of work; Gill ceased to be a registered architect in San Diego after 1920. Both Schindler and Richard Neutra, who for a time worked with him, had to struggle against legal restrictions which allowed only Spanish style houses in certain areas, against art juries composed of 'plain citizens', against obstructive building departments and against banks reluctant to advance loans.

Apart from Wright's 'textile block' houses, the late 'twenties in California produced some notable houses, nevertheless. Among them was Neutra's house for Dr. Lovell completed in 1927 and widely publicized outside the United States. With its light steel framing, its balconies and horizontal strip walls floating out on graceful cantilevers, the Lovell house combined the best qualities of the Californian 'skeletal pavilion' with the sophistications of European composition deriving from the cubist vision; it revealed too, a thorough knowledge of the kind of spatial exploration Frank Lloyd Wright had been making in his Chicago houses, and it is not surprising to find that Neutra worked for Wright on his arrival in America from Vienna in 1923.

The picture of architecture in America during the nineteen-thirties is at first glance one of stagnation. The depression hit the building industry with special severity, and when the economy began slowly to improve, revivalism in architecture seemed as powerful a force as ever. A heavily beporticoed neo-classical was favoured for low buildings like art galleries, libraries and government buildings, gothic of one kind or another (seldom well-versed) for high 'skyscraping' buildings, housing newspaper offices and the headquarters of chain-store empires, and neo-colonial, given a new lease of life by the reconstruction of Williamsburg, was widely used for the suburban house and the country house and club.

Above, Philadelphia Savings Fund Society, Philadelphia,
Pennsylvania, 1932, by Howe and Lescaze; a forceful expression
of the building techniques that made the skyscraper possible.

Above, Museum of Modern Art, New York City, 1939,
by Goodwin and Stone (the annex at the end was built in
1951 to the designs of Philip Johnson).

Below, McGraw-Hill Building, New York City, 1931,
by Raymond Hood.

Below, Daily News building, New York City, 1930,
by John Mead Howells and Raymond Hood.

But parallel, if sometimes all but invisible, the foundations were being laid for a rebirth of that architecture which had enjoyed such a short life at its first incarnation. In the words of James Fitch 'it is one thing to build a single thirty-storey skyscraper. . . . It is quite another to be able to reproduce them at will across the land. This required the raising of the *entire average level* of the building field.' The period from the close of the first world war through the 'thirties was one of rationalization in building; it saw a rapid development in the efficiency of mechanical services—elevators, electricity, plumbing, and air-conditioning—and a beginning of prefabrication. Though the 'thirties brought depression and a decline in building, it was also the decade which saw the rebirth of an architecture taking inspiration from building technology and from the aesthetic explorations of architects abroad. In the Philadelphia Savings Fund building by Howe and Lescaze, the Museum of Modern Art* by Goodwin and Stone, in the Kaufmann house and the Johnson Administration building by Wright, in houses by Neutra in California and Stone in New York State, an upsurge of creative vitality among architects was clearly being paralleled by a growing interest in their efforts by a section of the public.

Above, house at Belmont, Massachusetts, 1949, by The Architects' Collaborative; an example of the New England regional style evolved during World War II.

Even more important for the future of American architecture, education received a new stimulus with the arrival of distinguished architectural refugees from Europe. In 1937 Walter Gropius, who had been working in England since leaving Germany in 1934, was invited by Harvard University to take over its Graduate School of Design; Marcel Breuer joined him shortly after and there began a collaboration in teaching and building that was to have a profound influence. 'Few other schools of great architects', says Peter Blake, 'have produced so many excellent apprentices in so short a time.' The architecture that resulted, until some time after the second world war, mostly domestic, was a blend of the New England vernacular (white wood frame and great fieldstone fireplaces) with the highly sophisticated German manner of the 'twenties. It is remarkable for a meticulous attention to detail and, especially in the houses produced by the Gropius and Breuer partnership, for clarity in planning and a subtle understanding of the play of light and shade over white wood walls punctured with windows whose pattern owes much to the visual experiments started in the Bauhaus. These houses of the late 'thirties and early 'forties, as well as those produced afterwards by the two architects independently and by their students, form a body of work with its roots in a regional tradition of building and its growth fertilized by new ideas and ways of living, comparable to the domestic architecture of the California Bay Region. As distinct from the regional architecture of the Middle West they are hybrid styles, the one acknowledging a debt to the Far East, the other to Europe. The contemporary Middle West domestic architecture of such men as Wright, Goff and Schweikher was self-consciously American, expressing itself also often in wood, but with an even stronger sense of 'place', a sense of continuing tradition upheld by the longevity of Wright, and an individualistic conception of detail sometimes verging on the eccentric. Nevertheless it holds its place with ease as one of the three distinctive and lively American contributions to regionalism in twentieth-century architecture.

Above, house at Berkeley, California, 1951, built by Vernon de Mars for his own occupation; a skeletal pavilion of redwood and stone, on a steeply-sloping site.

Above, Colmorgan house, Glenview, Illinois, 1937, by Bruce Goff; oriental influence with a Middle West accent.

With the entry of America into the second world war a new impetus was

* A building destined to house an institution that has influenced incalculably the American public's understanding and appreciation of twentieth-century architecture.

Above, external facing of galvanized steel, Weirton Steel Company, West Virginia; typical of the anonymous industrial architecture which preceded the development of the curtain-wall.

Above, 505 Park Avenue, New York, by Emery Roth and Sons, showing the set-back to the upper storey dictated by daylight angles and codes.

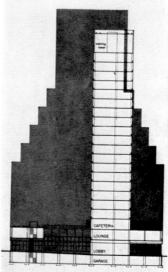

Above, section through the Lever building, the dark area shows the shape the building would have taken if it had filled completely its zoning envelope.

given to the rationalization of building methods. The urgent need for economy and increased speed of erection of buildings designed for the manufacture and housing of material for a war-time economy encouraged mammoth firms of architects and architect-engineers like Albert Kahn, Austins, and Giffels and Vallet to exploit to the full the advantages of prefabrication and 'dry' construction, largely in the form of sheet metal walls. This was an unselfconscious architecture not attempting any other effect than that which necessary repetition and essential scale gave it.

Studies in the application of new methods to war-time housing were of a different nature, and exercised the attention of such men as Neutra, Gropius and Wachsmann, Breuer, Koch and Stubbins. The ideas they produced were an important contribution to the problems involved in the layout, design and construction of the low-price family house. Two ingenious systems of prefabrication evolved were the General Panel Corporation's packaged house by Wachsmann and Gropius, and Carl Koch's folding Acorn house, but, due to the pattern the speculative building industry took in America after the war, these efforts bore little fruit, whereas the war-time methods evolved for industrial buildings vitally influenced the trend of post-war American architecture.

The early 'fifties in America saw a boom in down-town property values in many of the larger cities. In New York especially, hotels and apartment blocks were replaced by office buildings designed as a speculation and usually of anonymous character, with a wedding-cake outline arrived at by entirely filling the envelope dictated by daylight angles. More important were the office headquarters built by banks and other large business concerns, partly for purposes of prestige. The worthy tradition for this stretches from Sullivan's early skyscrapers through Wright's Larkin building, on past the unadventurous gothic grandiosities of the Woolworth Building and the Chicago Tribune Tower, the futuristic Chrysler and Empire State buildings, to the distinguished, if scarce, examples of the 'thirties like the buildings for the *Daily News* and the McGraw Hill Publishing Company.

In the interval between the last of these and the construction of Lever House, the necessities of war had revolutionized many building techniques and methods, the architectural 'umbrella' practice had developed, and the United Nations Secretariat, designed by an international committee of architects under the chairmanship of Wallace Harrison, had revealed to an appreciative public the unique charms of the all-glass curtain wall.

Though the idea and use of curtain walls can be traced to the beginnings of the modern movement—in the sketch schemes for all-glass towers of Mies van der Rohe and in buildings by Gropius, Behrens, Dudok and many others—their development as a marketed building product, their successful employment even as expensive and specially designed custom-built walls, had to await not only a public opinion to appreciate them, but also advances in the metallurgical and plastics industries, for there were many problems to overcome in waterproofing, insulation, and the expansion and contraction of the different materials involved. War-time needs directed attention to some of the technical problems, the United Nations Secretariat to some of the aesthetic potentialities, which, so far as the

Above, Heinz Vinegar Plant, Pittsburgh, Pennsylvania, by Skidmore, Owings and Merrill, a self-conscious and highly sophisticated essay in the industrial aesthetic.
Below, left and right, the United Nations Secretariat, New York City, 1950, by Wallace K. Harrison and an international board of design; the first building in the public eye to employ the all-glass curtain wall. The two photographs reveal the varied effects, according to the time of day or the angle of vision, of walls which from a distance and at first glance seem to stare back unwinking.

public was concerned, would seem to have been confirmed by the effect of the Lever building when it was completed in 1952. It is often forgotten that, apart from the hiatus in architectural progress inseparable from war, the immediate post-war period in America showed few signs of the creative vitality that has revealed itself since. The impact, therefore, of the elegant Lever building with its shimmering green glass and its aluminium trim, was the more powerful, and set off a chain reaction with effects that can be traced from San Francisco to the City of London.

The growth of the curtain wall industry that followed the popular success of the Lever building and the widespread use of its products by architects in America and Europe has brought a refreshing breath of anonymity where there had hitherto been an excess of self-expression, often with very little to express. Apart from the obvious advantages of the 'dry-construction' curtain wall for industrial buildings, the glass and sandwich-panel grid is clearly suitable for multi-cellular buildings like offices, laboratories and hospitals; however, the excitement of the initial impact has tended to encourage its over-enthusiastic application to building-types not always best suited to its properties. It would be unfortunate if this factor, together with insufficient attention to sun-control, were to start a reaction against a method of building which with its regular and repetitive grid has much to commend it in the urban landscape of today where a neutral backdrop can do much to tie together an environment often in danger of dissolving into anarchy.

In Mies van der Rohe, America has a poet, prophet and pace-setter in metal and glass architecture. Both he and his buildings stand somewhat apart from the commercial development for which he and the other visionaries of all-glass architecture are in large degree responsible. The Lakeshore Drive apartments and IIT buildings in Chicago, the Seagram building in New York, are the outcome of a lifetime of experience, of deep thought and long processes of experiment, concerned with the aesthetic and technical problems of metal and glass architecture. The result is often too subtle and indirect to make an immediate appeal to the public, and the value of a great architectural practice like that of Skidmore, Owings and Merrill as intermediary between poet and public, cannot be overestimated. In their chief designer, Gordon Bunshaft, they have a man well aware of all that Mies stands for, and in his buildings as well as many others produced from the offices of the partnership in four separate cities, can be found an application of Miesian principles which, though it may sometimes lapse into the platitudinous, often succeeds brilliantly in relating and even developing them within a broader architectural context than Mies's necessarily selective approach to existence is likely to bring him.

The growth of the 'umbrella' practice which may include within one partnership, architects, engineers, landscape and interior designers and many other specialists, is significant to American architecture in more ways than one. It is an inevitable outcome of the increasing complexity of building. It was foreshadowed before the second world war by firms of architect-engineers like Albert Kahn Inc., who rationalized the whole process of design and construction of industrial buildings. The adaptation of their methods to an architectural practice concerned to produce buildings

Facing page and right, two further views of the U.N. Secretariat; every tenth floor (indicated by grilles) houses the mechanical services, which are so important and costly a part of the contemporary building in America.

Above, the U.N. Secretariat seen in relation to the General Assembly building.

Above, the Lever building from Park Avenue.

Above, the Alcoa Building, Pittsburgh. Below, the Socony Mobil Building, New York.

of high architectural quality has not only accelerated appreciation of what the new architecture stands for and is capable of encompassing, it has set new standards of office procedure for other, smaller, architectural firms, thus contributing to a higher respect for the architectural profession among clients, many of whom rate efficiency a good deal higher than design ability.

The developing rationalization of building and office practice, the industrialization of building components, and the increasing acceptance of air-conditioning as a necessity instead of a luxury are ironing out regional distinctions. So far, the architecture of the private house is less affected by this than other categories of buildings. Even the 'built-for-sale' house, for which a large measure of prefabrication is sometimes employed and which might be expected to reflect this, is often dressed in a regional costume quite unsuited to its climate and the company it keeps. The 'Prairie House', for instance, is frequently to be found far removed from any accessible prairie. Big building operators like Levitt or adventurous, smaller ones like Eichler in California, are still a long way from developing an aesthetic of rationalized house-building of the kind envisaged in schemes by Gropius and Wachsmann or Buckminster Fuller.

It would seem to be the opinion of many of the architects whose work is surveyed on the pages that follow that the decline of distinctive regional character in architecture is considered inevitable, given the potentialities and demands of our time, and that such a decline need not mean an overall loss of variety in architecture so much as a shift of emphasis, with variety deriving from the honest solution to the design of different building types and from the different handwriting of the various architects at work. They see, it would seem, the whole nation as a region with climate influencing architectural expression only in those categories of building not yet affected by air-conditioning.

It has long been the cause of concern that the mechanization of building would lead to uniformity, an endless repetition of standard box-like units bringing an end to character and the expression of the creative personality. It is now clear that this need not be so. The day is not far away when industrialized countries able to produce factory-made frame buildings will also be able to construct, both on-site and in the factory, moulded buildings, without the expensive and time-devouring methods that complex reinforced concrete design requires, and which make of it a luxury where labour costs are high. The use of plastics and sprayed concrete will give architects a sculptural freedom never known before, a freedom that for many of them raised, as they have been, largely within a rectilinear system of aesthetics, presents some formidable new problems. Lacking discipline and a rigorously controlled imagination the new freedom could lead to form-making for its own sake—an unbridled mud-pie architecture. Buildings like Le Corbusier's Chapel at Ronchamp and Frank Lloyd Wright's Guggenheim Museum in New York, both by men who have spent their lives exploring the sculptural potentialities of the new architecture, foreshadow the opportunities and the difficulties ahead of us.

The mid-'fifties mark an interim attempt to explore a richer vocabulary of form for certain kinds of buildings. Under the influence of engineers like Candela, Nervi, Weidlinger and Salvadori, architects like Saarinen,

Left, Alcoa Building,
Pittsburgh, Pennsylvania,
1955, by Harrison and
Abramowitz; the thin-gauge
dished-aluminium sheets
were prefabricated in floor-to-
ceiling panels (see below);
the round-cornered windows
pivot for cleaning, are
pneumatically-sealed when shut.

Right, assembly of the outer
facing of the U.N.
Secretariat—glass in the long
walls and Vermont marble on
the short ones.
Bottom of the page,
prefabricated thin-gauge
stainless steel panel, Socony
Mobil Building, New York,
1956, by Harrison and
Abramowitz (see also facing page).

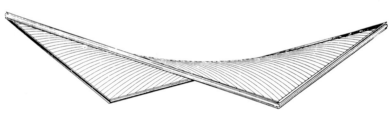

Above, project for a stadium to seat 99,000 spectators, by Raymond and Rado; Weidlinger and Salvadori, engineers; the bowl is constructed of tension-rings in concentric circles, overhanging 150 ft. without support; the roof is of shell barrels tapering towards the centre.

Eelow, restaurant and supper club; bottom, concert pavilion; both part

Above, drawing of the hyperbolic-paraboloid wood roof for a house at Raleigh, North Carolina, by Eduardo Catalano; Attilio Gallo, engineer. The main advantages of a warped plane of this kind are: 1, though doubly-curved it can be made of straight members; 2, all stresses are equal (no bending moment); 3, stresses are calculable; it is very rigid.

Below, State Fair Arena, 1952–53, by William Henley Deitrick in association with Matthew Nowicki; Severud-Elstad-Kruger, engineers. The roof is supported on cables stretched between a pair of inclined reinforced concrete arches supported on steel columns at 8 ft. centres.

of a master plan for Long Beach, California, by Raymond and Rado, in association with David Leavitt. The structure of the restaurant is a concrete hyperbolic-parabaloid shell composed of three diamond-shaped arches springing from three steel pivots. The concert pavilion is a double-arched concrete canopy springing from two points in the ground.

Raymond and Rado, Catalano, Stubbins and Yamasaki have produced structures which give the roof a new lease of life. Curved and folded shells, hyperbolic parabaloids, membranes suspended from portal frames and arches, cover airports and congress halls, houses and night clubs, sometimes seeming to be chosen for their own sake, rather than for the sake of the building sheltering under them. They are evidence nevertheless of vitality in American architecture and a willingness to take risks in order to conquer new fields of expression. These, sometimes, halting steps forward, may prove to have been useful training when the new materials and methods are perfected and 'sculptured' form becomes cheaper and easier to construct. It is unlikely that they will replace present systems of rectilinear construction which, with their standardized components and mechanical equipment, will continue to be refined and improved for multi-storey buildings. It may be that this rectilinear architecture will provide the neutral backdrop against which the freer sculpted forms of the concert hall, the building for worship, the sports drome, the transport concourse, can act as foil and foreground incident.

It is still early, though, to talk of any large-scale planned effects of this nature in the American urban, or suburban, environment. The flight from city to suburb of families and their attendant service industries, the move of many commercial and industrial concerns to the countryside where land values are less, labour often cheaper and conditions of work healthier, has imposed a new pattern on the map and created building types like the suburban shopping centre, the full implications of which have not yet been fully explored. The problem it poses for cities whose loss of revenue can clearly be traced to their inability to cater for family life and the universally-used motor car, has led to some hard thinking. Cities like Fort Worth, Pittsburgh, New Haven and Denver, are producing plans and instituting programmes of reconstruction which may revitalize the concept of life in down-town America. Except on paper and but for schemes under the control of one private developer or municipality, realization is as yet piecemeal and unco-ordinated. There is little, outside rehousing projects, on the scale of the pre-war Rockefeller centre. Civic improvement during the last ten years has seldom gone beyond the provision of a small piazza here and there—like those round the Lever and Seagram buildings—though the Lincoln Center for the Arts is indicative that in New York as in many other cities, impatience is growing at the twentieth-century's failure to provide itself with an urban environment it can be proud of.

The opportunities for architects in all this are immense, though in few countries, as yet, does their training fit them for tasks that involve entirely new problems of scale, of reconciliation between the old and the new, of the reintegration of all the furniture and equipment that is an inescapable part of the modern city, to produce a coherent picture which strikes the right note between order and anarchy. However, in one of the skills needed American architects have lately shown themselves adept. During the period of its establishment and growth the new architecture was, understandably, isolationist. There was much that could not be accomplished in a spirit of compromise; the demands made, for instance, by a situation calling for architectural tact and an understanding of factors such as arise in renova-

Above, roof-elevation and eye-level view of a model for a supper-club at Santurce, Puerto Rico, by Torro and Ferrer in association with Charles H. Warner, Jr.; the structure is a thin shell of reinforced concrete (3 in. thick at the crown).

Above, a projected beach-house in Cuba, by Philip Johnson, with a vaulted shell-concrete roof and pierced-screen walls.

Above, house project by John MacL. Johansen; the structure is concrete sprayed on to an armature of steel pipe, rod and fabric. Below, the Monsanto house, part of a research project into the uses of plastics in building; the structure is moulded plastic panels 8 ft. by 16 ft., bent to form ceilings, walls and floor, cantilevered in pairs from a central utility core.

tion and renewal where a clean sweep is impracticable, factors which call for diplomacy in addition to strongly held convictions, were demands which, if they had been met too readily and too soon, could easily have deflected the new architecture from its path and opened the way for yet another era of reaction. It is a sign of maturity, therefore, that these problems can now be considered dispassionately by both the middle and younger generation of architects. In extensions to existing groups of buildings like Paul Rudolph's Art Center at Wellesley College and Saarinen's library block at Chicago University, in the number of Embassy buildings abroad where an attempt has been made not only to take into account climatic differences but also the prevailing character of each place, as reflected in the scale, colour, texture and materials of its architecture past and present, experience is being gained which will benefit America when it comes to realize the great schemes of reconstruction now being planned. Though realization may still be some way ahead, given a continuation of the progress shown during the last fifteen years, the new American architecture will surely justify the faith of Louis Sullivan who considered nothing less than a balanced and vital environment in town and country worth striving for.

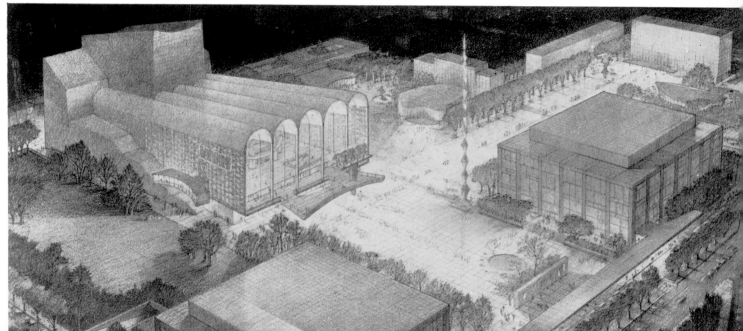

Louis Sullivan

Louis Henri Sullivan forms a bridge between the ground-clearing pioneers of the modern movement in America, like H. H. Richardson, and those who, like Frank Lloyd Wright, began to build on that new ground an architecture not merely clean, bold and fresh in its externals, but renewed to the marrow of its bones by the fusion of a down-to-earth approach to design with revolutionary materials and techniques.

Like Richardson, he had a Beaux Arts training, though it served mainly to reinforce his objections to all he saw in it that was false; like Wright (who when his turn came rejected a Beaux Arts training out of hand), and unlike Richardson, he had an instinctive grasp of the great opportunity offered to the architect by new structural techniques, in particular those connected with the use of steel.

Born on September 3, 1856, in Boston, Massachusetts, he spent most of his summers on a farm belonging to his maternal grandparents at South Reading, where he developed a love for nature and organic form which was to find expression in the exquisite drawings for the stone and metal carving that later embellished many of his buildings. It was in the English High School in Boston, under the direction of Moses Woolson, that he received his first real discipline in learning, and it revealed in him a variety of aptitudes, for languages, for mathematics, for history and philosophy, all of which were to stand him in good stead when he took in 1874, after only six weeks' preparation, the rigorous examination of the Ecole des Beaux Arts.

Meanwhile, in the year 1872, Sullivan attended the courses at America's first architectural school, the Massachusetts In-

Above, part of the ornamental cast-iron sheathing which surrounds the entrance and display windows of the Carson, Pirie, Scott store, Chicago, Illinois, 1899–1904. The design was detailed by Sullivan's partner Elmslie and then modelled in plaster by Kristian Schneider.

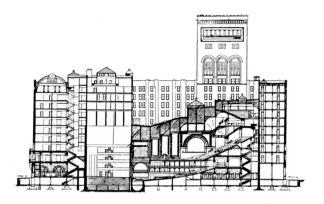

Top, longitudinal section through the Auditorium Building, Chicago, Illinois, 1887–89, by Adler and Sullivan. Above, oblique view of the façade on the tower side. The offices of Adler and Sullivan (where Wright also worked) were on the floor of the tower with the recessed, pillared openings.

stitute of Technology, founded six years before. He left without finishing, and while visiting an uncle in Philadelphia, saw and admired a building by Frank Furness. He applied for and got a job in the Furness office, where he worked until the depression of 1873, when he moved on to Chicago and once again chose an office to work in with characteristic perspicacity, this time with William Le Baron Jenney, an engineer-bon-vivant and the first man to build an all-steel frame building.

After his two years at the Beaux Arts Sullivan returned to Chicago, working as draughtsman in various offices until, in 1879, he joined Dankmar Adler. At the age of twenty-five, in 1881, he was made a partner, and during the next twelve years the firm of Adler and Sullivan was one of the most active in Chicago. It was a well-formed partnership, Sullivan the 'designing' partner, Adler the engineer-constructor—dependable, liberal, far-seeing—with a growing clientele and in need of just the sort of man that Sullivan was. Together they landed one of the most important commissions of the time in Chicago, that for the new opera house known as the Auditorium building and including an office block with a great tower destined to house the headquarters of Adler and Sullivan on its seventeenth floor.

In Sullivan's own words, the Auditorium was 'the culmination of his masonry "period" ', and it was completed in 1889. In the decade 1880–1890 the population of Chicago had doubled itself to a million (from a mere 4,000 in 1837). It was a boom city, full of pride and self-assurance and with a powerful urge to build high. There was a limit, however, to the height attainable with solid masonry construction. Burnham and Root's sixteen storey Monadnock building needed walls at ground level twelve feet thick, and the practical Chicago building promoter could well understand the wastage involved in such a factor. 'The Chicago activity in erecting high buildings finally attracted the attention', Sullivan tells us, 'of the local sales managers of eastern rolling mills; and their engineers were set at work.' The mills for some time past had been rolling those structural shapes that had long been in use in bridge work. . . . The need was there, the capacity to satisfy was there, but contact was not there. Then came the flash of imagination which saw the single thing. The trick was turned; and there swiftly came into being 'something new under the sun'.

As Colin Rowe has shown us, in Chicago the steel frame answered a specific need of clients and architects who, at least in the field of business building, were practical men first and patrons of the arts and aesthetic innovators second. In

Europe the steel frame acquired for the modern movement something like the symbolic importance of the quarterings on a shield; but for the Chicago architects, it remained the simplest, cheapest and boldest method of constructing the tall, multi-cellular office block. As a result the lack of self-consciousness of these buildings gives many of them an impressive directness and force of expression.

In Sullivan's first essays in the frame structure, the Wainwright building, St Louis, 1891, the Guaranty building, Buffalo, 1895, and the Bayard building, New York, 1898, he was concerned, as most of his Chicago contemporaries were not, to investigate 'psychological expressiveness' in the façade of the frame building, with particular emphasis on vertical stress. In the process he created buildings which have widely influenced American architecture and, in their masterly assurance, successfully deflected attention from Sullivan's more subtle and infinitely more important frame building, The Carson, Pirie, Scott department store, Chicago, of 1899–1904. In the latter building Sullivan was not so much

Top right, Wainwright building, St. Louis, Missouri, 1890–91, by Adler and Sullivan. Right, Guaranty building, Buffalo, New York, 1894–95, by Adler and Sullivan. Above, Bayard Building, New York City, 1897–98, by Louis Sullivan. In the Wainwright and Guaranty buildings Sullivan was at pains to arrive at a suitable form for the multi-storey office building; both are masterful statements by a great architect but the formula was seldom to prove so successful in the hands of other architects, though many used it. In the Bayard building, which Sullivan himself preferred, the unsupporting verticals read plainly as mere window mullions, whereas in the Wainwright and Guaranty buildings they are made of equal thickness to the structural columns.

concerned, one feels, to achieve 'psychological expressiveness' as he was to refine and perfect the simple, unselfconscious, and sometimes naïve, designs of the practical men. In this he succeeded and arrived, in the words of Sigfried Giedion, at 'the neutral and impartial equilibrium inherent in cage construction'. It was an impressive swan-song, whose theme was not to be taken up again until, half a century later, Mies van der Rohe focused the attention of the architectural world once again on the Chicago frame, this time though with many additional subtleties and sophistications accruing from Mies's European background and numerous technical advances that had been made in the interval in the metallurgical industries.

Various suggestions have been put forward to explain the failure of the new architecture to flourish in Chicago just when it seemed so successfully to have taken root. The force

Facing page, above, Carson, Pirie, Scott store, Chicago,
Illinois, 1899–1904, by Louis Sullivan; a remarkable
design which has retained its freshness over sixty years.
Here the plan requirements of a department store
suggested a horizontal rather than a vertical emphasis in
the façade, but it is not stressed unduly and the general
effect is one of even balance which, though it was never
a prime consideration with Sullivan, does reflect the
nature of the frame structure.

Facing page, below, Gage building, Chicago, Illinois,
1898–99, by Louis Sullivan (Holabird and Roche,
Assoc.); one of three units, two of which were by
Holabird and Roche (the centre one shows in the left of
the photograph). Sullivan's unit is faced with terracotta
and his 4 ft. high continuous windows are surmounted
by panels of translucent glass.

Above right, exterior, and below, interior, National
Farmers' Bank, Owatonna, Minnesota, 1907–8, by Louis
Sullivan. The first of the banks built by Sullivan in the
latter part of his career. The arched windows are 36 ft.
in diameter with double-glazing and a hermetically-
sealed air space between; the inner window is of
opalescent leaded glass. Exterior materials are of brown
sandstone, dark red brick, enamelled terracotta in
bronze-green and brown with a five-inch band of blue,
green, white and gold, glass mosaic.

of the Beaux Arts example was certainly strong, especially in the east, and since the Committee on Buildings and Grounds of the 1893 Chicago World Fair was made up of five architects from the east and five from the west, it is not entirely surprising that Beaux Arts principles carried the day. But it was not only in the realm of aesthetics that the east was making itself felt; in the business world many of the independent concerns of the middle-west were merging with those of the east to form trusts, cartels and monopolies. On top of all there was only one architect of major stature, Louis Sullivan, who really believed in the new architecture; the others, as we have already seen, were practical men producing the 'goods' desired in the quickest and most economical way; when the desire for a different type of goods arose they were perfectly prepared to satisfy the new desire, cheaply or expensively. The strength of Chicago's golden age of commercial architecture was, therefore, also its weakness, and the ideals of one man, powerful as they were, became a pathetic irrelevance in face of a sudden and largely uneducated demand for the trappings of a borrowed culture.

With uncanny accuracy Sullivan prophesied that 'The damage wrought by the World Fair will last for half a century from its date, if not longer.' He was, of course, aware that it was a symptom of reaction, rather than a cause of it; nevertheless, the Chicago World Fair of 1893 both confirmed and popularized a taste for a foreign style, not connected, as the Greek had been, with ideals of young nationhood, and successfully blinded a generation of Americans to a native gift that was just beginning to emerge and prove itself. For Sullivan it was a personal defeat, and after 1900, although he lived until 1924, his career was virtually at an end. A number of small banks were built, but considered in the light of his whole work and of the fact that they were almost the sole product, apart from his autobiography, of twenty years, they serve to emphasize the nature of the tragedy that overtook this great man.

Frank Lloyd Wright

Frank Lloyd Wright is America's eldest and greatest practising architect. His working life spans nearly three-quarters of a century, starting in Chicago in 1887 whence he came as a student of engineering from the University of Wisconsin. Of Anglo-Welsh ancestry, the Unitarian faith was a powerful force on his mother's side of the family and (in spite of the prophet Isaiah for whom the young Frank conceived an antipathy) it proved formative of more than his literary style. The natural beauties of Wisconsin where, during his 'teens, Wright worked on his uncles' and aunts' farm, instilled in him an almost pantheistic fervour which has never left him and to which can be traced his concern to be at one with the site, to see that his buildings were not merely 'on' the ground but 'of' it. In some measure too this may explain his love of natural materials and his hymning of the 'organic' in architecture, which is an article of faith to be honoured from the kernel of the creative process through to the last stone, brick and doorstop.

A brief survey of a life so long and so incredibly fertile can select only a few examples and a few of the principles from which they developed. Fortunately the life and its works have been and continue to be documented and described by Wright himself as well as by historians, critics, commentators and littérateurs.

Not long after his arrival in Chicago, Wright joined the firm of Adler and Sullivan, then working on the first important building the partnership was to produce, the Chicago Auditorium. The young architect rose within three years to become head of the drawing office and conceived, during this time, an affection and respect for the great Louis Sullivan which has never left him and whom he still calls 'Lieber Meister'. By 1893 when he set up on his own in Oak Park, a suburb of Chicago, Wright had already produced an outstanding work as a member of the firm (the Charnley house) as well as a number of houses designed in his 'spare time', a difference over the definition of which was the cause of his temporary break with Sullivan.

Through the suburbs of Chicago during the next ten years until 1910, Wright fought a lone struggle to establish new concepts of domestic architecture. The Willits house of 1902 is an early example which reflects these concepts with clarity and conspicuous success.

Wright was concerned to achieve a free flow of interior

Above, Charnley House, Astor Street, Chicago, Ill., 1891, designed in the office of Adler and Sullivan, but now known to have been largely the work of Wright.

Above, the living-room of the Coonley House, Riverside, Ill., 1908; note the breaking down of the 'room box'—the free flow of interior space.

Above, Willits House, Highland Park, Ill., 1902, 'first masterpiece among the Prairie houses'.

Left, Robie House, Woodlawn Avenue, Chicago, Ill., 1909; the ground-hugging horizontal lines are reminiscent of the Prairie which gave these houses their name.

space by breaking down the room 'boxes' in which people confined themselves (though he submitted to the necessity of four walls for a bedroom). He aimed at a closer relationship not only between the outdoors and the in, but also between the building and the ground on which it stood. Among his means to the attainment of these ends were the continuous casement window and (inside the house) the bringing of the ceiling by various devices of colour and material down the walls to the window transom, which projected outside as an overhang, producing a ground-hugging, stream-lined effect, following the line of the Prairie that was to give this type of house its name. The nature of these houses is as of a complex abstract pattern in negative and positive, the outer forms interlacing, the inner spaces interpenetrating, the one the complement of the other.

Some of this the architects of the Atlantic seaboard had already achieved (see page 13), in houses of the 'Shingle Style', especially the freer handling of interior space. But the totality of the Wright house of this period was unique, and in the Coonley house of 1908 and the Robie house of 1909 he was to produce two masterpieces which have now gained recognition as such, though the latter was recently saved from destruction only through an international campaign of protest.

Meanwhile, in 1896, on the farm where Wright had first rebelled against and then accepted the rigours of hard manual labour, and for the same aunts, he designed a windmill which forecast his structural ingenuity and provided him with a leit-motif, 'The engineers said I couldn't do it, but I did'.

Three other buildings of the period forecast three further interests which were to prove lifelong. Francisco Terrace of 1895 was a first essay in the problem of low-cost housing, and though there were to be few opportunities for field experiments in the subject it was not for lack of theories and projects.

The Larkin Building in Buffalo built in 1904 for a large mail-order business forecast Wright's interest in the new social problems of American commerce, and his understanding of the architectural challenge it offered. Here was a building that grew directly out of the working and recreational requirements of a large clerical staff. It was fireproof, easy to maintain and admitted plenty of daylight; it was also the first building of its kind to be a standing protest against the squalor of the American commercial landscape; by turning the building in on itself, centring it around an oblong glass-roofed court rising through its whole height, and placing all external windows above eye level, it created an interior space of independent interest. It was for the Larkin Building that Wright designed the first metal office furniture and the first wall-hung w.c.

The third of these prophetic buildings was the Unity

Above, Windmill at Spring Green, Wisconsin, designed by Wright in 1896 for his aunts.

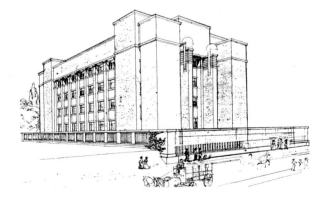

Above, Larkin Building, Buffalo, N.Y., 1904, designed for clerical work; the interior has offices ranged round a glass-roofed court.

Above, Midway Gardens, Chicago, Ill., 1914. A pleasure garden in which Wright combined sculpture, painting and architecture to form a masterly and unified composition far ahead of its time.

Above, Imperial Hotel, Tokyo, Japan, 1916–22. A monumental work of earthquake-proof construction, built of reinforced concrete and brick, with lava sculpted to Wright's designs.

Above, Millard House, Pasadena, California, 1923. The first of the 'textile block' houses made of pierced concrete blocks and reinforced cement fill. Left, detail of relief pattern blocks on the Millard house.

Temple, Oak Park, of 1906, a pioneer effort in the development of modern concrete construction. Aside from forecasting Wright's skill in handling new materials (or old materials in a new way), Unity Temple was remarkable as a building moulded to and moulding the low church service, and with heating and lighting elements an integral part of the architectural effect.

The Midway Gardens of 1914 gave Wright the opportunity to design on the symphonic scale. A pleasure garden the eighteenth-century English would have called it and, with its three acres of terraces, loggias, galleries and restaurants, it brought into full play Wright's by now mature decorative ingenuity, his complex 'spacemanship', his ability to conjure up his own *genius loci* where no worthwhile one existed, to produce what must have been a magic setting for an evening out. But it was far in advance of the community for which it was made and declined into a beer-garden, finally closing with Prohibition and being demolished within less than a decade.

Great personal tragedy intervened at this period of Wright's life and, hounded by notoriety, it must have been with relief that he accepted the commission to build the Imperial Hotel, Tokyo. Now famed for the way in which it withstood a dramatic earthquake soon after its completion, the Imperial Hotel is an immense structure of brick, concrete and lava, the last sculpted in Wright's very personal idiom and illustrating his ready acceptance of *matière trouvée*. The primary means evolved by Wright (and the engineer Paul Mueller, formerly with Adler and Sullivan) to ensure the structure against earthquake shock was the cantilever. The floors of the flanking bedroom wings, for instance, were supported entirely on the corridor walls, in the manner of a tray on a waiter's fingers, as Wright put it, merely interlocking with but not resting on the external walls. Great pools of water in the courtyards were there for purposes of fire prevention as well as decoration. All came into play in the earthquake and the fire which followed, fully justifying the forethought that had been given.

During the time that the Imperial Hotel was building, between 1916 and 1922, Wright made several visits to California, where he built some houses employing a system of precast concrete blocks, patterned, sometimes pierced and with metal rods running vertically and horizontally between them in hollows which were then filled with cement. The Millard House in Pasadena, 1923, is an especially fine example of what are known as 'The Textile Block Houses', and it exhibits a fresh and entirely apt expression for domestic architecture in

Above, model of the projected, but never built, Press Building, San Francisco, 1912. Below, and facing page, Taliesin West, near Phoenix, Arizona, 1938, but still building, the winter headquarters of the Taliesin Fellowship. Materials are canvas screen and timber truss rising from a canted base of red desert stone set in concrete.

a region very different in climate and vegetation from Wright's own mid-western habitat.

The 'twenties saw some pioneering skyscraper projects of a more radical nature than the 1912 scheme for the San Francisco Press Building. The National Life Insurance Building, Water Tower Square, Chicago, 1924, had it been built, would still have been in advance of its time in 1950. It was a double cantilevered structure with an external sheathing of copper and glass hung from the edges of the floors. But this period for Wright was one of much hope and thought but little fulfilment, and the depression years were to be leaner still.

Work continued, however, on his own headquarters at Taliesin, Wisconsin. Started in 1911 on land given him by his aunts, Taliesin I was destroyed in the tragic fire of 1914. Taliesin II grew from the ashes, to be burnt, in its turn, in the 'twenties. Taliesin III was started in 1925; it still continues as Wright's summer home and the centre of the Taliesin fellowship. It is an extensive, low-lying group of buildings in wood and local stone, which of all Wright's work melds most closely with the site: indeed from some angles it appears literally to grow out of the ground.

The winter headquarters of the fellowship, known as Taliesin West, at Scottsdale, Arizona, was started in 1938 and is a masterpiece of romantic abstraction in stone, wood and canvas. The prototype for it was Ocotillo Camp, built in 1927, near Chandler, Arizona, to provide living and working space

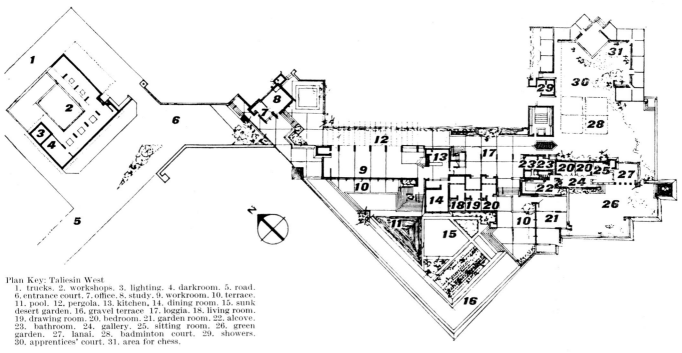

Plan Key: Taliesin West
1. trucks. 2. workshops. 3. lighting. 4. darkroom. 5. road.
6. entrance court. 7. office. 8. study. 9. workroom. 10. terrace.
11. pool. 12. pergola. 13. kitchen. 14. dining room. 15. sunk
desert garden. 16. gravel terrace 17. loggia. 18. living room.
19. drawing room. 20. bedroom. 21. garden room. 22. alcove.
23. bathroom. 24. gallery. 25. sitting room. 26. green
garden. 27. lanai. 28. badminton court. 29. showers.
30. apprentices' court. 31. area for chess.

for Wright and his assistants while building San-Marcos-in-the-desert, a large resort centre, never to be realized.

Wright's major work during the years of the depression was the privately sponsored regional planning scheme known as Broadacre City, a scheme for life based largely on agricultural and industrial smallholdings, remarkably at variance with the actual structure of the American economy, though consistent with Wright's personal philosophy.

In 1936 for the Kaufmann's, Wright built what is, perhaps, his most widely publicized house, Falling Water, Bear Run, Pennsylvania, a system of immense cantilevers poised with astounding drama over a waterfall. The same year saw the beginning of the Johnson Administration Building at Racine, Wisconsin. Recalling the Larkin building in the way it creates its own interior landscape, it grew, however, out of very different structural principles, ones evolved by Wright in his effort to break free of post and beam construction, with its right angles and sharp edges. The Johnson Building is a wrap-around brick and tubular-glass skin, with interior space created by a series of piers blossoming out into continuous

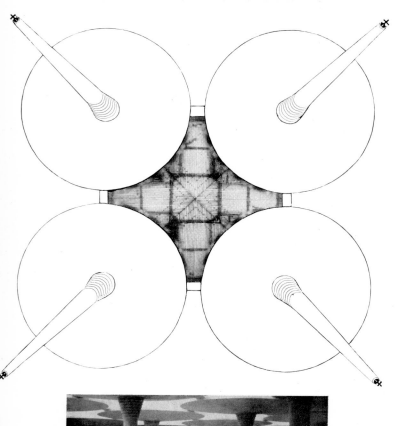

Top left, tubular glass wall in the administration wing (1936–39) of the Johnson building at Racine. Middle left, diagrammatic drawing of the piers which form the administration hall showing the glass tubes filling the space between the 'lily pad' caps. Bottom left, general view of the hall with the mezzanine balcony beyond. Below, Unitarian church at Madison, Wisconsin, and right, facing page, Frank Lloyd Wright demonstrating the symbolism of the church with his hands.

'lily pad' tops to form the ceiling; in the great administration hall, the interstices are filled with tubular glass providing an aquarium-like light; the spatial effect of this hall is such as to place it very near the top of Wright's architectural achievements. In 1949–50 there was added a laboratory block in the form of a tower with floors cantilevered out from a central cylinder.

From 1937 onwards, numerous houses were built to a system of partial site-prefabrication devised to cut the cost of medium-sized houses. They are called Usonian (Usonia being Wright's synonym for the United States of America) and employ plywood sandwich panels for exterior and interior walls and wall-high doors which are also windows; the roofs are supported on crossed two-by-fours on four-foot or five-foot centres, the alternative modules on which all the plans and elevations of these houses are based.

The major work in hand during the 'forties was Florida Southern College; this is a complex of buildings constructed of cement blocks and providing a contrast with the flat site by the powerfully-faceted modelling of the higher buildings

Above, Chapel at Florida Southern College, Lakeland, Florida; started in 1938 the college buildings, constructed of poured concrete or pre-cast blocks, are situated on a flat site among citrus groves.

Left above, interior of the Morris Shop, San Francisco, 1947, with its spiral ramp and glass 'bubble' ceiling. Left, arched entrance to the shop, which has a blank façade of brick with raked joints. Below, tower project of 1929 for St. Mark's-in-the-Bouwerie, New York, prototype of Wright's later tall buildings.

such as the Memorial Chapel and the Library; building work on the College still continues.

Recent years have brought Wright many commissions, and buildings by him are being erected all over the United States. In 1955, the opportunity at last came to realize a project of 1929 for St Mark's-in-the-Bouwerie, New York, a cantilevered mast structure similar to the Johnson Laboratory; the result, known as the Price Tower, is a nineteen storey apartment and office block entirely of reinforced concrete and sheathed in copper and glass, situated in Bartlesville, Oklahoma.

The latest of Wright's major works is the Guggenheim

Above, Price Tower, Bartlesville, Oklahoma, 1956; a realization of the ideas embodied in St. Mark's tower project of 1929. The structure is reinforced concrete partially sheathed with prefabricated copper panels. Above right, the Guggenheim Museum of Non-Objective Art, Fifth Avenue, New York, 1943–58, of poured and sprayed concrete in the form of a great cantilevered spiral which is itself the main picture gallery.

Museum of Non-Objective Art on Fifth Avenue, New York, nearly opposite the Metropolitan Museum. Built of reinforced and of sprayed concrete, the main gallery is in the form of a spiral ramp, the radius increasing as it mounts. Visitors will take a lift to the top and walk down with pictures on one side of them and, on the other, a great interior space rising ninety feet from floor to glass-domed roof.

In his eighty-seventh year nobody would now question Wright's claim to greatness. His literary oeuvre with all its repetitions, its occasional obscurity and sometimes inadequately reasoned criticism of the theories it opposes, its paradoxes and contradictions, is a strange but noble literary achievement in its own right. Like the man's architecture, it defies comparison as completely as it defies emulation. This is far from saying that Wright's architectural influence has not made itself felt, but wherever it has been fruitful, it is in matters of general principle rather than of detail. He stands as one of the great geniuses of architecture, and uniquely so in that he had to create his own style, his own philosophy and his own tradition single-handed, unsurrounded by even near-equals, and in the early years unrecognized beyond the immediate confines of 'Chicagoland'. With half-a-century's perspective, the exploration and assessment of Wright's early work still proceeds; it may be as long again before a precise evaluation can be made of the significance and influence of his whole achievement.

Mies van der Rohe

Mies van der Rohe, at the age of seventy-three, and a long way from his native Aachen, has become, for many among the middle and younger generation of architects, the living embodiment of a moral absolute. Quite what this is they would most of them find it hard to define, and since architecture seldom prospers alongside moral absolutes, it is just as well. What they do see quite clearly is a poet of metal and glass, of the fine edge and the moulded profile, above all a master of the rectilinear in plan, elevation and volume and in the relationship of building to building. His approach is opposite to that of Frank Lloyd Wright and no two buildings could better exemplify the difference than the two masters' first major works to be built in New York which have risen, by a coincidence, almost simultaneously. No. 375 Park Avenue (the Seagram building) is sheathed in autumnal bronze; crisp and rectilinear it soars to the sky without emphatic termination. The Guggenheim Museum on Fifth Avenue is curvaceously moulded, ground-hugging, even ground-penetrating with a spiral terminated by a glass dome, reading as much downward as upward. The two buildings represent the polarities of modern architecture, metallurgy and the machine serving the purposes of the multi-cellular building, on the one hand, and the structural versatility of reinforced concrete used to make a formal statement about a unique problem, on the other; both approaches are as valid as they are necessary.

However true it may be that the famous Lake Shore Drive towers are the fulfilment of the dream of a glass skyscraper that had exercised Mies in Berlin as early as 1919, however true it may be that he is 'always the same Mies', the fact remains that his coming to America in 1938 marks a real break in his career, and his American architecture is very unlike that which he had earlier done in Europe. The earlier body of work had consisted mostly of small buildings and large projects—except for the Weissenhof-seidlung of 1927, but, as Germany's intellectual life contracted towards the null-point of 1933, even small commissions became scarce and it was left to Mies, as its last director, to turn the key on what remained of the Bauhaus—and on what remained of an adventure, a generation, a dead world. In its own good time the New World offered him the chance to realize his large projects; offered him

[continued on page 57

Above and facing page, Farnsworth House, Plano, Illinois, 1950. 'A study in the relationship between supporting and supported elements.' Eight steel columns are welded to the outside of the *fascias of roof and floor which with the steps and deck are given the appearance of 'floating' above the site. Floors are of Italian travertine, and the continuous curtains of raw silk.*

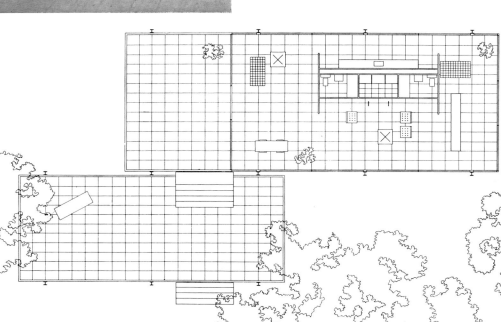

Above, below and facing page, 860 Lake Shore Drive, Chicago, Illinois, 1951. Two twenty-six storey blocks of flats, whose relationship is shown at ground level in the plan on the left. Far right, facing page, plan and section through wall and key elevation.

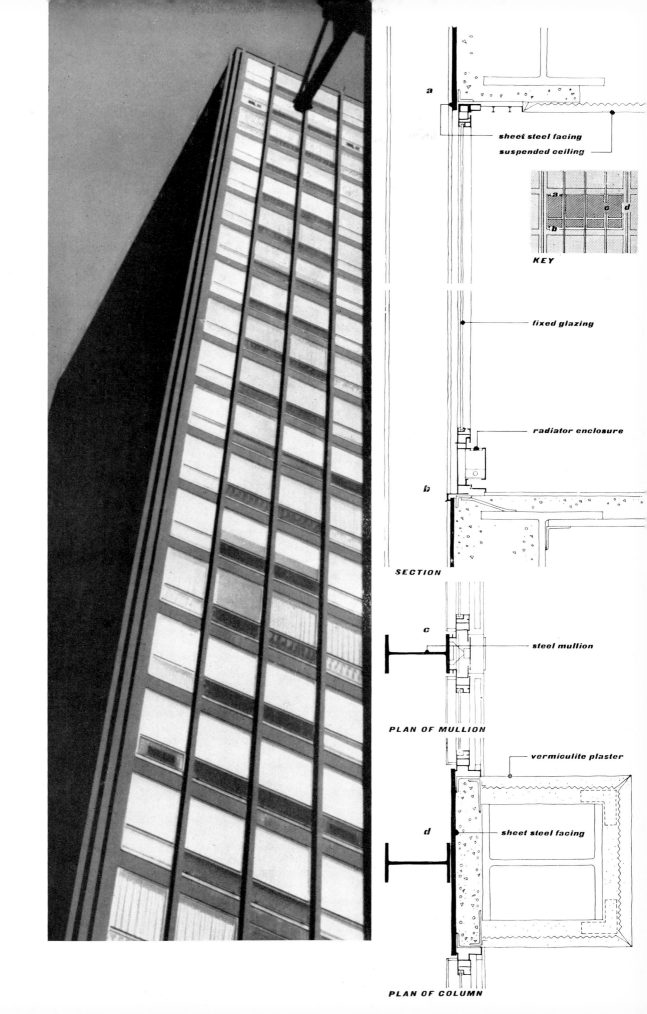

a

sheet steel facing

suspended ceiling

KEY

fixed glazing

radiator enclosure

b

SECTION

c

steel mullion

PLAN OF MULLION

vermiculite plaster

d

sheet steel facing

PLAN OF COLUMN

Above left, the two blocks at 860 Lake Shore Drive, looking towards the lake. The external glass skin is carried between I-section steel mullions at 5 feet 3 inches centres; each fourth mullion coincides with a main structural stanchion; above right, a section of the mullions and spandrels being hoisted into position. Below, left and right and top, facing page, views of the Lake Shore flats showing how light strikes the carefully profiled mullions producing endlessly varying effects at different times of the day. Below right, facing page, the Commonwealth Promenade Apartments, Chicago, 1957, where Mies has replaced steel, used for the earlier Lake Shore buildings, with aluminium for mullions and spandrels.

*Above, Esplanade Apartments, Lake Shore
Drive, Chicago, 1957. This further pair of
buildings are beside the 1951 blocks; they are
similar in design to the Commonwealth
Apartments (previous page) and like them have
grey-tinted glass walls; unlike them the aluminium
mullions and spandrels are anodized black.
Below and bottom, facing page, Crown Hall,*

*designed for the architectural department of the
Illinois Institute of Technology, Chicago, 1957;
an early model of the layout of the Institute is
shown top left, facing page. Top right is a detail
of one of the buildings completed in 1947,
photographed in 1950 to show the effect of
matured planting on Miesian architecture.*

continued from page 50]

the necessary patrons, the materials, the techniques, the engineers and collaborators—and the IIT campus, as its buildings were completed one by one over the years on his twelve-foot planning grid, revealed to US architects an extreme point in architectural integrity, a right rectangular aesthetic of structure and space. This aesthetic, summed up in two basic Miesian sayings, *Wenige ist Mehr* and *Beinahe Nichts* (Less is More, and Almost Nothing) has been called the 'Absence of Architecture', but on a middle generation of Americans it has reacted as a positive presence, and as Mies has gone on developing it, refining and subtilizing its structural forms and

[*continued on page* 60

Above, model for the Cullinan Hall extension for the Museum of Fine Arts at Houston, Texas, which has a familiar Miesian structure of brick, steel and glass, but a curved plan, which is rare among his recent work.

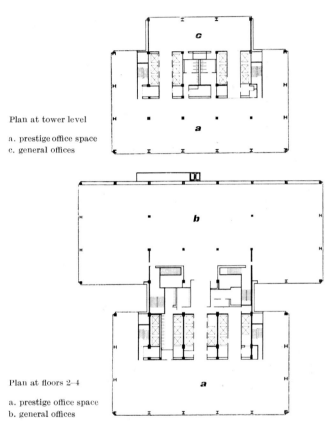

Plan at tower level

a. prestige office space
c. general offices

Plan at floors 2–4

a. prestige office space
b. general offices

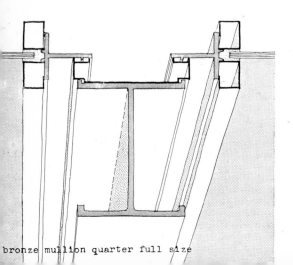

bronze mullion quarter full size

Left and facing page, details and photographs of 375 Park Avenue, New York (the Seagram Building), 1958, by Mies van der Rohe and Philip Johnson. But for the grey-tinted glass and granite panels, the whole exterior—mullions, windows and spandrel panels—is of bronze. Left and facing pages are details showing connections between the main structure and the curtain wall. Spandrel panels shown during installation, bottom facing page, are of rolled sheet bronze. Above are floor plans.

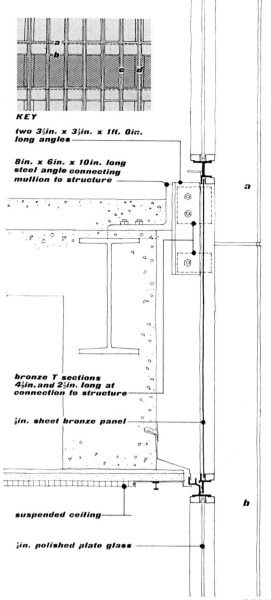

KEY

two 3½in. x 3½in. x 1ft. 0in.
long angles

8in. x 6in. x 10in. long
steel angle connecting
mullion to structure

bronze T sections
4½in. and 2½in. long at
connection to structure

⅛in. sheet bronze panel

suspended ceiling

¼in. polished plate glass

a

b

SECTION

c

PLAN OF MULLION

d

PLAN OF COLUMN

continued from page 57]

formal structure, a giant ghost has followed it at a safe and not-quite-comprehending distance—the curtain wall industry. For, though Mies's achievement could hardly be more personal, the superficial appearance of the buildings in which that achievement is embodied has facilitated the visual acceptance of a repetitive, endless, grid façade, while the work of two architects most ready to admit his influence, Eero Saarinen and Gordon Bunshaft, has effectively bridged the gap between one man's vision and an industrial product.

America could not have nurtured Mies, Europe could not have fulfilled his promise; he has, perhaps, gained more, and given more, to the US than any other *émigré* outside the realm of atomic physics. He has produced a lyricism of two constituent US psychological facts—unlimited space and unmitigated technology—in a form that is neither provincial nor crude, and can be held up to the rest of the world as an example of a convincing machine-age architecture. The rest of the world has taken note and, wherever architectural thought is on the move, the influence of Mies—American Mies—can be felt.

The completed forty-two storey skyscraper, 375 Park Avenue. Below, view of the entrance hall at night from the opposite side of Park Avenue; the walls enclosing the lifts are faced with travertine and brilliantly lit. Facing page, the completed building by day with the Lever building appearing to the right of the photograph. At night 375 Park Avenue is lit through all its floors as part of a preconceived architectural effect. The piazza on the Park Avenue side, like the Lever one, opposite, is a gift to the city of New York by the building owner.

Richard J. Neutra

Richard J. Neutra, almost alone of America's leading architects, has tangled at many points in his career with the great names of the Modern Movement. Born in Vienna in 1892, he studied with Otto Wagner and came under the influence of Adolf Loos. In the early 'twenties he shared an office with Erich Mendelsohn in Berlin, and like Mendelsohn and Raymond Schindler (another Viennese) he soon crossed the Atlantic and headed for Chicago and there met Wright and Sullivan. Unlike Mendelsohn, who returned to Berlin, he stayed on long enough in Chicago to help nurse Sullivan through his last illness, and then followed the path that Schindler had pioneered to the Pacific Coast.

It was a classic education in Modernism which he was soon passing on to such rising talents as Harwell Hamilton Harris and Gregory Ain. Ever since then, his rigorous and imaginative attitude to technology (which has its roots in the Neutra family tradition) and his thoughtful attitude to the psychology of architectonic form (which has its roots in his readings of Wundt) have gained and maintained for him a solid reputation on both sides of the Atlantic, while the basic attitude which he derives from these interests is summed up in his dictum 'Constructed human environment should be an entity, and not split up by specialists'.

Both in his writings and his buildings he has shown a remarkable consistency over the years—works of 1927, like the Lovell House, and of 1955, like the Brentwood Gemological Institute, are unmistakably Neutra, even though they also bear witness to a careful and pondered architectural development.

Below, entrance to Richard Neutra's own house and office, Silver Lake Boulevard, Los Angeles; a pioneer experimental building of 1932. Below, middle and right, a recent community building by Neutra, a Teenagers' Club at Eagle Rock, California.

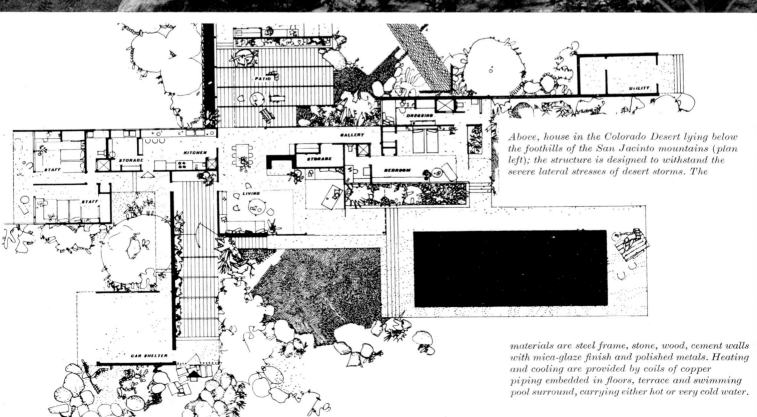

Above, house in the Colorado Desert lying below the foothills of the San Jacinto mountains (plan left); the structure is designed to withstand the severe lateral stresses of desert storms. The

materials are steel frame, stone, wood, cement walls with mica-glaze finish and polished metals. Heating and cooling are provided by coils of copper piping embedded in floors, terrace and swimming pool surround, carrying either hot or very cold water.

SCALE IN FEET
0 5 10 15 20 25

Above, a house by Neutra of brick and timber,
a rare combination of materials for him; it is at
Brentwood, California, and this view over the
pool is from the south west. Left, plan, and
below, the owner's bedroom.

*Above, Tremaine House, Santa Barbara,
California, view towards the car port and
entrance. The structure is of reinforced concrete
with panel walls of coursed rough stone. Below,
the west terrace looking towards the living-room.*

Below, offices at Los Angeles, California; this façade, since it faces south, is filled with a movable aluminium brise soleil which is illuminated from below at night. Top, facing page, one of the office interiors; below, the carefully devised planting which is on both sides of the ground-level glazed wall.

Below, house at Bel-Air, California; view from the nook. The dining space is on the left, and the living-room and terrace to the right of the Texas shellstone fireplace.

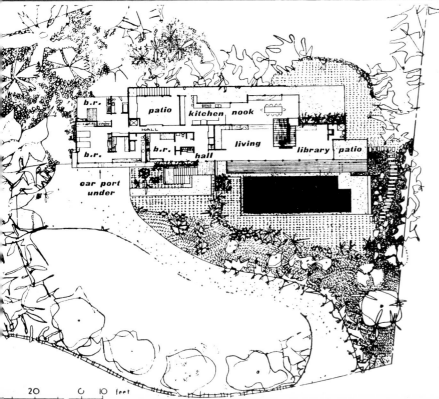

Above, house at Bel-Air showing the first floor patio at the end of the library-living-room wing, with changing rooms for the swimming pool below; plan at left.

b.r.

patio   kitchen   nook

HALL

b.r.   b.r.   hall   living   library   patio

car port
under

20   0   10   feet

Left, constructed human environments
by Neutra; above, a view-facing
extrovert house at Ojai, California;
below, a courtyard-facing introvert house
at Eel-Air, California.

William Wilson Wurster

William Wilson Wurster was born at Stockton, California, in 1895; it was a town of 30,000 people in the Great Central Valley of the San Joaquin, and Wurster's father would take him on each bank holiday (he worked in a bank) to see some new aspect of it. Starting with a fire station, a foundry, a mill and leading through to the City Hall, County Court House and the offices of the local newspaper, until he got to know how the town worked in all its details. He decided to be an architect at the age of three, guided, he thinks, by his mother, who had been impressed by his question 'How do chimneys stay on roofs?'

During High School he worked in the summer for E. B. Brown, an English architect in Stockton, a gifted, irascible and unbusinesslike man, but it was a good office to be in, and the work had character and style.

He went to the University of California in 1913 to study architecture under John Galen Howard; however, health and the First World War broke in and he didn't finish until 1919. At architectural school Wurster remembers himself as a conformist, and the whole group, prior to the 'twenties, missed the 'modern surge', though, even then, façadism made him uneasy.

The first office job after qualification was in San Francisco with an honourable, tight-fisted architect of Scottish descent; he obtained his work as a brother-in-law of the mayor, but his performance was beyond reproach. It was not, however, a gay office. Wurster left to work for Charles Dean in Sacramento on an engineering project; there he learned all the field things fast, designed and built three houses on the side, saved $4,000 in two years and in 1922 set off for a year in Europe.

On his return he worked in New York with the firm of Delano and Aldrich until 1924, when he moved back to the

Top, reading from left to right, the partnership of Emmons, Wurster and Bernardi. Above, the Gregory Farmhouse, an early commission that won a House Beautiful award in 1927; below, the Stern Hall Dormitory at the University of California.

Above, the Nowell House, Stockton, California, 1953, one of Wurster's more formal designs in the Bay Region idiom. Below, the Monterey Public Library, 1952; bottom, plan of the Ford Foundation's Center for the Advanced Study of the Behavioural Sciences, Stanford, California; right, is a reading room in one of the blocks marked 8 on the plan.

Bay Region, starting his own office in 1926. One of the earliest commissions was the Gregory Farmhouse, designed in one day; it was carpenter architecture (a protest against the, then popular, Spanish stucco) and when it won the second House Beautiful award in 1927 Wurster was 'off to the races'. He now has two partners, Theodore Bernardi and Donn Emmons; sharing the office are mechanical and structural engineers who have other clients as well.

Wurster's chief admirations are Alvar Aalto (in architecture), Barlach (in sculpture) and Cézanne (in painting); he regrets that his clients usually seem to prefer Cadillacs. A constant source of inspiration has been his fellow-townsman Maybeck, and Wurster sees in his Fine Arts Palace (San Francisco) and Christian Science Church (Berkeley) the embodiment of what he considers an ever-relevant dictum—'Let's use the past and yet be free.'

Plan Key:

1. administration
2. library
3. seminars
4. meetings
5. lounge
6. dining
7. kitchen
8. study groups

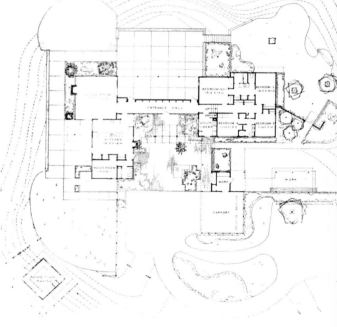

Top, view from the north-east towards the living room and kitchen terrace area of Wurster's Dawson house, Los Altos, California, 1958; left, kitchen and above, plan; the house is of wood frame construction faced with vertical redwood boarding.

Above, Buckminster Fuller under a dome at Woods Hole, Massachusetts, while beyond a helicopter lifts a prototype of his magnesium, Marine Corps dome.

Richard Buckminster Fuller

Richard Buckminster Fuller, born in 1895 in Fulton, Massachusetts, and with a New England Transcendentalist background (his aunt, Margaret Fuller, with Emerson, founded and edited *Dial*, the organ of Transcendentalism), is an engineer, mathematician, inventor, designer, mechanic, writer and philosopher, a 'Comprehensive Designer' he calls himself.

He is the only man in this book working well beyond the boundaries of the architectural profession, but for all that, or because of it, no book on contemporary American architecture should omit him. He is one of the freshest and most inspiring of educators in architecture, a thinker who has invented his own system of geometry (Energetic and Synergetic geometry [Sy-en. for short] were discovered by him in 1917); and he has applied it to the problems of mass shelter to produce entirely revolutionary concepts of structure.

Through apprenticeship with a group of cotton mill machine fitters and later, in the meat industry with Armour & Co; through concentrated attention towards getting the 'maximum gain of advantage from minimal energy input'; through a deep concern over the inadequacy of the building industry and the inattention of the architectural profession to

Fuller's Dymaxion—maximum performance with maximum economy—prototypes. Upper left, the Phelps-Dodge moulded bathroom unit; left, the Dymaxion car; and above, the Wichita house of 1946.

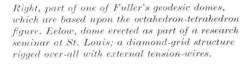

Right, part of one of Fuller's geodesic domes, which are based upon the octahedron-tetrahedron figure. Below, dome erected as part of a research seminar at St. Louis; a diamond-grid structure rigged over-all with external tension-wires.

*Left, one of the semi-expendable
Marine Corps paper-board domes seen airlifted.
Middle and bottom, below, a geodesic dome
unlike most of the others with structure and cover
separate; the 55 ft. three-quarter sphere has a
homogeneous structural skin composed of 363
standard plastic elements which are bolted to the
frame; it is designed to withstand extreme
temperatures and wind-loadings up to 200 m.p.h.*

the matter of satisfying the needs of the world's sub-housed
millions, Buckminster Fuller evolved his philosophy, his geometry, his techniques, and out of them a string of prototypes
for mass-production in the fields of shelter and transport. In
the Wichita House of 1926, in the Dymaxion House of 1927,
and in the Geodesic Dome, he has shown himself one of the
few men alive today who can straddle specialisms to produce
viable and entirely new solutions to the problem of optimum
space and amenity at minimum cost. As yet his prototypes
have proved too far ahead of their time to be generally accept-
able, except in the military field where so often our fears lead
us to welcome technical advances we are too lazy to put to use
for humanitarian ends or too hidebound to put to use for our
own benefit, especially if they conflict with the prejudices that
centre on the idea of Home.

Above, the all-aluminium—144 ft. diameter and 57 ft. high—dome constructed by the Kaiser Aluminum Co. and erected in 20 hours by 38 men for a resort auditorium in Honolulu to seat 1,800 people.

Right and below, the Union Dome, Baton Rouge, Louisiana, seen under construction; 375 ft. in diameter (the world's largest), the dome is made of folded, and externally-braced hexagons of steel sheet; it shelters the repair and maintenance shops for a tank-car company.

Pietro Belluschi

Pietro Belluschi comes from Ancona, in Italy, where he was born in 1899. He passed, by way of training in Rome, and a degree in civil engineering at Cornell, to the office of A. E. Doyle in Portland, Oregon, which he served as chief designer from 1927 until the firm was dissolved in 1943. He then set up his own practice, but this, in turn, no longer exists as a normally constituted office and since he was made Dean of Department of Architecture at MIT, Belluschi has worked as a roving consultant in design, especially in the fields of church architecture, shopping centres, and office buildings. His work in these three fields is so dramatically dissimilar that he eludes routine evaluations as an architect in terms of style—whether personal or generalized—and he has been appreciated mainly for his achievement in building up a position in which he can design buildings that command respect in the often deadening

mental climate of a provincial city—though in this respect Portland is as a-typical as he is. But the stylistic adaptability is as integral a part of his make-up as the community-conscious, for both are aspects of what he calls 'the kind of integrity that breeds variety as nature will have it'—nature in this instance clearly subsuming the character of the community as well as the building's function.

His churches and houses, wood-framed, wood-clad, and often likened to local barns, were early in the field of 'redwood vernacular' and were taking circumspect note of Japanese architecture as long ago as 1938. On the other hand, his business buildings, square, smooth and sharp-edged, include in their number the Equitable Building of 1948, which anticipates much of what was later to be done at UN and Lever House.

Below, house at Yamhill, Oregon, built round a courtyard with a separate guest house. The structure is wood frame faced outside with rough-sawn boards and battens. Left, living room exterior and porch; right, living room hearth.

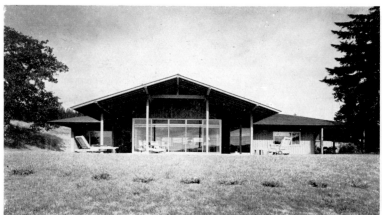

Above and right, Equitable Savings and Loan
Building, Portland, Oregon; an early example in
American office buildings (1948) of the reflecting
surface; by bringing glass, mullions, transoms
and spandrel panels into the same plane as the
polished aluminium facing of structural columns
and beams, the architect gave this building some
of the characteristics of the later sheath-type
curtain wall (see Lever Building, page 134).

Right and below, First Presbyterian Church, Cottage Grove, Oregon; the exterior of the frame structure is rough-sawn fir boards and battens; interior walls are plaster or spruce. The view on the right is of the Chapel which is open at all times for prayer or meditation.

Above, First Lutheran Church of Boston, Back Bay, Boston. The church is set on a small site, in a crowded district of brick Victorian buildings, and had to be designed from the inside out; materials are brick and timber. Below, perspective of the design for Temple Israel, Swampscott, Massachusetts, which is shown as completed overpage; it was designed in association with Carl Koch and Leon Lipshutz.

*Left above, view towards the sanctuary of
Temple Israel, Swampscott, Massachusetts; the
hexagonal form of the sanctuary derives its shape
from the Star of David; folding doors connect
it to a large auditorium. Materials are pierced
walls of brick, glass, and redwood which is
lacquered on the inside and stained on the outside.
Left below, interior of the sanctuary showing
the supporting structure of laminated wood.*

Louis Kahn

Louis Kahn was born on the island of Osel in Estonia in 1901. His father was an artist and a worker in stained glass; his mother, a harpist. Kahn started to draw at an early age and during his 'teens won annual prizes, finally being offered two scholarships at the Philadelphia Academy of Fine Arts; instead, at the age of sixteen, he decided to be an architect, and chose to study at the University of Pennsylvania.* His first job was in the office of the Philadelphia city architect where he was put in charge of design for the Sesquicentennial Exposition of 1926 but, in his own words, he 'simply applied the stylistic design-making tendencies of the day to a unique problem of spaces and communications in a made-up world' —a lost opportunity he wishes he could have over again.

He next went to the office of Paul Cret (who was head of the University of Philadelphia's architectural department), where the assistants were so many sorcerer's apprentices, re-

*Music is Kahn's other interest and he could have had a scholarship to study that too, for the asking.

Above, first stage of a public housing project in the Mill Creek area of Philadelphia; building began in 1953.
Below, AFL-CIO Medical Center, Philadelphia, a central clinic for union members. The structure is reinforced concrete; the massive beams have hexagonal perforations designed to house duct runs. The exterior is faced with polished granite.

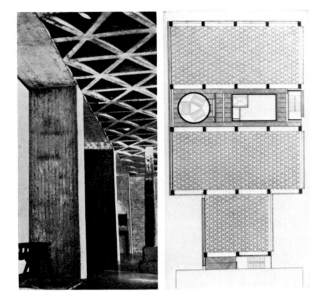

constituting under the master's watchful and educated eye, ingredients from old Beaux Arts recipes.

The first independent job was a small synagogue, the second the original unit of a psychiatric hospital; both came from clients who must have felt, he thinks, that a young man would give them more for their money. On top of his practice, Kahn now teaches at Yale and the University of Pennsylvania.

Louis Kahn believes that architecture begins with 'the thoughtful making of spaces'. 'Organic' qualities in architecture stem from an intuitive understanding of order, the order of spaces, of structure, of building, of services, of movement, all taken separately and together. Forms that come ahead of thought about space interfere with the development of its organic qualities. 'Standardized' architecture implies, he considers, 'stabilized means, static space and accepted function'.

'Space is architectural when the evidence of how it is made is seen and comprehended. A single span space with intervening non-structural partitions raises the question as to whether it is meaningful form when shorter spans could be truer to the nature of the spaces. An "order-concept" of space could inspire the design of structurally defined spaces that

Above left, detail of tetrahedral ceiling and unfaced concrete columns, and right, ceiling plan of the Yale Art Gallery, New Haven, Connecticut, 1955.
Right, sketch model for a tower resting on a 700 ft. square piazza. The structure demonstrates the predominant influence of horizontal wind forces over the forces of gravity in the design of high buildings.

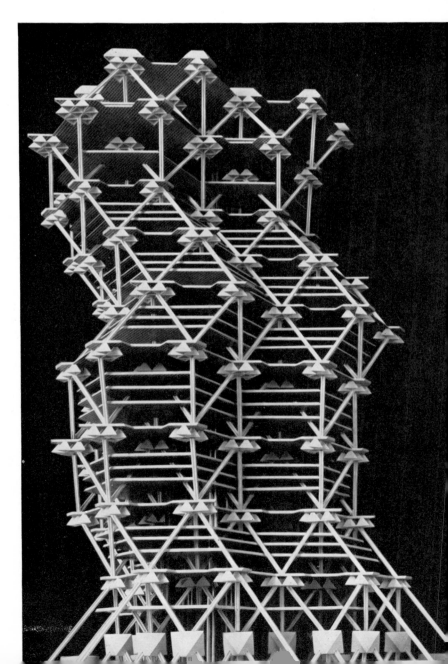

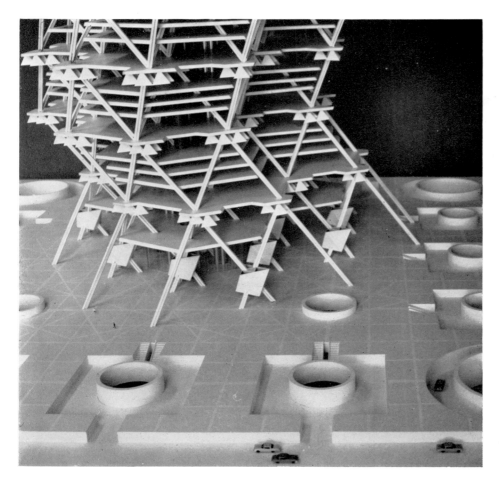

Left, view of the tower base and part of the piazza, the squares at one level lower than the main piazza are pedestrian entrances from the street and have escalators entering them from the car park below.

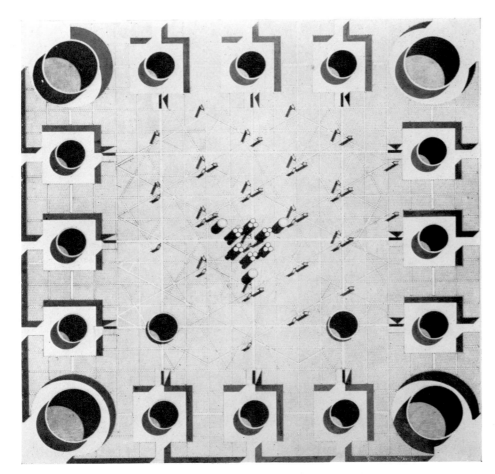

Left, plan of the piazza; the circular openings provide light and ventilation to the car park and shopping concourse beneath the piazza; cars enter and leave at the four corners of the site.

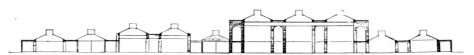

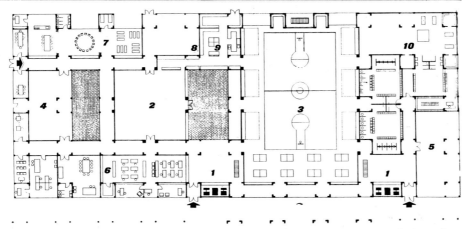

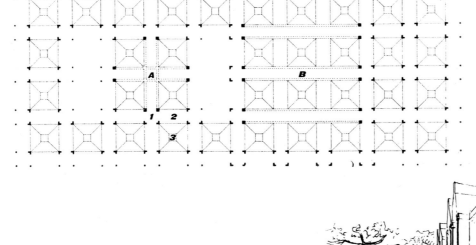

Left, section, model, ground, roof and column plan of a community centre for Trenton, New Jersey. Ground plan key: 1, lobby; 2, social hall; 3, gymnasium; 4, adult lounge; 5, youth lounge; 6, administration; 7, nursery unit; 8, shops; 9, kitchen; 10, turkish bath. Column plan key: 1, column centre space 11 ft. by 11 ft.; 2, oblong connecting space 11 ft. by 22 ft.; 3, major space 22 ft. by 22 ft. Below, sketch of the revised roof design for the connecting spaces.

"serve" and are "being served"; the large, the intimate and even the smaller voids in a structure (see Yale Art Gallery) should be inherent in that order-concept.

'The continual renewal of architecture comes from changing concepts of space. Long ago, when the walls parted and became columns, architecture began. Are there signs of another transformation, equally far reaching? Are glass, steel and reinforced concrete enough to inspire a new era in architecture? The changing nature of space suggests constant beginnings in architecture.'

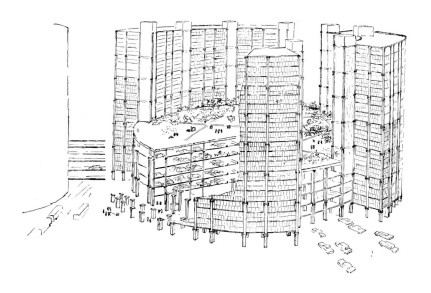

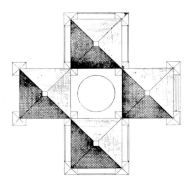

*Above, part of Kahn's proposals for the replanning of down-town Philadelphia; this shows one of the 'harbour' blocks which also provide a gateway to the city centre. The core is the car-harbour-parking-space, surrounding it would be offices, apartments and shops, facing on to an upper level piazza. Right, roof and ground plan and, below, view from centre of a bath house adjoining a swimming pool in Trenton, New Jersey, 1955. The hollow columns are 8 ft. square and are the servant areas of the major spaces. **Plan key:** A, women's dressing room; B, **men's dressing room;** C, basket room; D, atrium; **E, lounge;** 1, pool director's kiosk; 2, entrance to chlorinating equipment; 3, lavatories.*

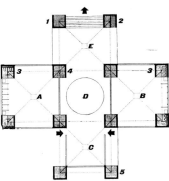

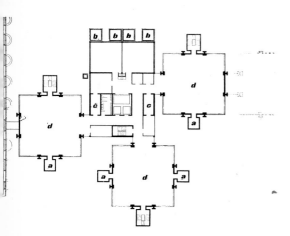

adapted for other purposes; the rest of the building
is shown continuing in dotted lines to the right.
The structure is reinforced concrete with brick
infill; corner beams have two-way cantilevers,
echoed by stepped-up windows.

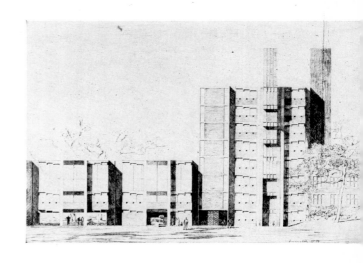

*Above and right, Science building, University of
Pennsylvania, Philadelphia. On the typical
upper floor plan at left, a, encloses the exhaust
ducts for laboratory gases as well as the service
piping; b, four nostrils for fresh air intake which
start at the third storey (above motor car exhaust
level) and distribute air downwards to the
laboratories; c, air ducts for central circulation
area; d, 45 ft. by 45 ft. free laboratory space,
capable of being subdivided according to need or*

Edward D. Stone

Edward D. Stone was born in Fayetteville, Arkansas, in 1902, and had a brother, James Hicks Stone, also an architect, with a practice in Boston. His earliest architectural recognition came at the age of twelve, when he won a first prize of two dollars and fifty cents in a Birdhouse competition. Five years later, the sight of New York from Brooklyn Bridge fired him to make his own contribution to the New York scene—an ambition that came to significant fruition in the Museum of Modern Art, which he designed in collaboration with Philip Goodwin, in 1939. Between the decision and the realization, he studied at the University at Arkansas, Harvard and MIT, and travelled in Europe on a Rotch Scholarship, designed the Radio City Music Hall, pioneered modern domestic design in the Eastern States (Mandel Residence, 1930) and established his own office in New York, in 1936. The firm is still called *Edward D. Stone*, Architect, and has no partners or associates, but there are now subsidiaries of the New York office in Fayetteville and Palo Alto.

*Above left, the Mandel house, Mount Kisco,
New York, 1930.
Above right, design for a 400-room, ten-storey
hotel at Karachi, Pakistan.*

*Above, drawing of the nursing wing of the Palo
Alto Medical Center, Stanford University,
California.*

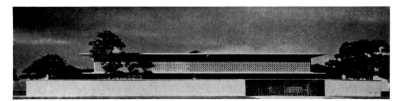

*Above, the Graf house, Dallas, Texas, surrounded
by a solid garden wall and with a pierced screen
wall at first floor level for sun protection.*

Since the war Stone's work has become—in a very conspicuous sense—representative of American architecture, since he has designed a number of important buildings and projects outside the US, notably the hotels El Panama (in Panama) and Phoenicia (in Beirut) and another one projected for Karachi, the US Embassy in New Delhi (which Frank Lloyd Wright suggested be called the Taj Maria, in honour of Stone's wife), the US pavilion for the '58 Brussels exhibition, and a large hospital in Lima, Peru. At home, the Palo Alto

[continued on page 94

Top left, facing page, cutaway elevation and model of a design for the Huntington Hartford Museum, New York; the whole building would be surrounded by a pierced bronze screen.

Left, facing page, model of the U.S. embassy at New Delhi, India. The structure is of reinforced concrete with an outer row of gilded steel columns, a double roof, a pierced sun-screen wall of tiles and an interior water-garden court with suspended strings of aluminium discs to give the effect of sunlight filtering through leaves. The whole building is raised on a rectangular platform with entrance for cars and parking space below it.

Right, Edward Stone's own house in New York City; a converted brownstone similar to the one remaining on the right of it; the tile screen is a prototype for the Delhi embassy opposite.

Left, the United States Pavilion at the Brussels Exhibition, 1958, at dusk. Through the transparent walls of the pavilion the lights can be seen picking out the open steel and aluminium ring suspended 60 ft. above the central pool.

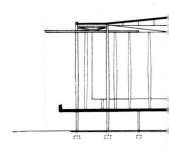

Above, close-up of the 'hub' of the 330 ft. diameter roof to the main U.S. pavilion at Brussels; the principle of construction is similar to that of the bicycle wheel; the 'hub' was made in the form of a double skinned steel drum 25 ft. high and 62 ft. in diameter (see section top right); this was assembled on the ground and then lifted slightly above its final position; steel cables were run from the top and bottom of the 'hub' to the surrounding wheel (which thus became a compression ring) and these were then allowed to take the weight. The lower cables were then draped in steel mesh suspended from the top cables, and translucent plastic panels were laid across the top cables on steel purlins. The walls of the pavilion which ran between a double row of metal pipe columns supporting the outer ring of the roof 'wheel' were of vinyl chloride set in a mesh of diagonally braced metal bars.

continued from page 90]

office is particularly flourishing, with a large volume of institutional building in California in hand. With so much tropical and sub-tropical work in the office, it is hardly surprising that the pierced screen and deep eaves should be almost the trade-marks of Stone's work at present, and it may be these qualities that earned him the rarely-dispensed admiration of Frank Lloyd Wright—'a young man with a brilliant future' were the Master's words. This admiration is reciprocated, and he also admires the work of Alexander Calder (which he used in his Arkansas university buildings), Henry Moore, Matisse, the town-planning of Bath, Piazza San Marco and Baroque Rome.

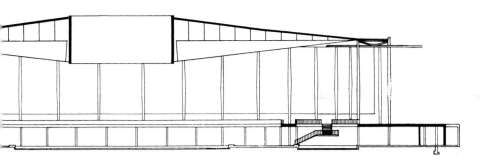

*Right and below, offices and plant for the
manufacture of vitamins and antibiotics,
Pasadena, California. The screened façade is of
white concrete and is 400 ft. long. Right, two-
storey inner atrium; employees' cafeteria is in the
court and the reception lounge is on the gallery.*

Marcel Breuer

Marcel Breuer, outstanding product of the Bauhaus's most brilliant period (1920–24) and designer of its most famous artifact (the steel tube chair), was born in Hungary in 1902, and decided to become an architect in 1904. After his Bauhaus training, and a phase when he combined headship of the Bauhaus interiors department with independent design-work outside, he passed by way of the Isokon network (which also handled Gropius and Moholy-Nagy) and collaborations with F. R. S. Yorke in England, to the USA in 1937, to team up with Gropius once more, teaching at Harvard, and partnering him as an architect. He was thus among the spearheaders of full, European modernism in US Academic circles and in New England house-building, and he has left his mark in both fields.

In house-design, however, he has made his deepest impression since the partnership with Gropius was dissolved in 1941, particularly with his 'Butterfly' exhibition house for the Museum of Modern Art, which was visited in 1949 by more

Left, facing page, and above, the first house that
Breuer built for himself in Connecticut. The
construction is based on the traditional American
'frame-type' house (see diagram on right); the
upper floors are cantilevered out 10 ft. at each
end of the house; the porch is suspended from
steel cables anchored by turn-buckles and belts of
a type used in the rigging of boats.
Below, Grieco house, Andover, Massachusetts,
a typical example of the Breuer manner with its
boarded exterior and wire-braced sun-shade.

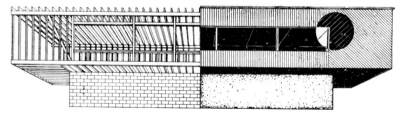

*Facing page, above, 'butterfly-roof' exhibition
house for the Museum of Modern Art, New York.
Facing page, below, house at Ligonier,
Pennsylvania, showing the living room exterior
and the stairs leading to the roof terrace. Stone
walls are local shale and wood sheathing is of
cypress: plan below.
Top left, Arts Center for Sarah Lawrence
College, Bronxville, N.Y., with its dance studio,
right, under the rake of the auditorium floor.
Above left, monastery wing of St. John's Abbey,
Collegeville, Minnesota, with the abbot's reception
room on the right. A model of the new church for
the abbey of St. John is shown overpage.*

than 70,000 people, and probably did as much as anything to
sell split-level sections to the US public. Epoch-making as
this may have been in the context of US housing at large, in
the context of his own work it was only one of a series of remarkable houses produced by him between 1945 and 1955,
houses marked by an extensive, original and authoritative
employment of wood and stone. The successes of this period,
and the very high quality of the work he put into them,
focused attention on him as a house-architect more than anything else, but he had always possessed the abilities and am-
bitions for larger work, and in the very middle of his house-
period he designed a dormitory for Vassar and the Arts
Center for Sarah Lawrence College. Since then projects and

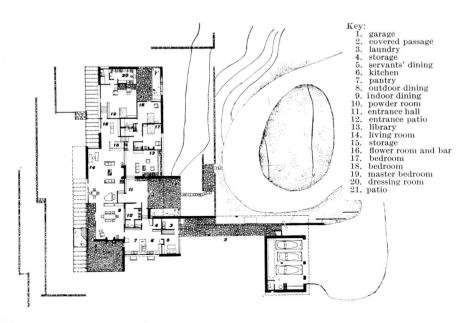

Key:
1. garage
2. covered passage
3. laundry
4. storage
5. servants' dining
6. kitchen
7. pantry
8. outdoor dining
9. indoor dining
10. powder room
11. entrance hall
12. entrance patio
13. library
14. living room
15. storage
16. flower room and bar
17. bedroom
18. bedroom
19. master bedroom
20. dressing room
21. patio

Above, Ereuer's present house at New Canaan,
Connecticut.
Below right, colour and letter symbols, designed
by Ereuer of the New Haven railroad.
Bottom, St. John's Abbey, Collegeville,
Minnesota, looking past the free-standing
reinforced concrete belfry to the glazed end-wall
of the church.

Above, model of a new library block for Hunter College, New York, with folded-slab reinforced concrete roof supported on central columns.

work in hand outside the domestic field include schools and college buildings, a factory, a monastery and two widely-discussed designs done in collaboration with Europeans in Europe, the UNESCO buildings in Paris, with Zehrfuss and Nervi, and the new *de Bijenkorf*, Rotterdam, with Elzas. As might be expected from one of the Bauhaus's star pupils his work is unforcedly personal, but never individualistic, and—as might also be expected of an old Bauhaus student—he has a distinguished roster of collaborators from the other arts.

Below, gable wall (with classroom wing to the left) of the gymnasium at Litchfield High School, Connecticut; the external wall is of diagonal wood siding.

Above left, temporary site office erected during the construction of the de Bijenkorf store in Rotterdam, shown above right, and facing page. The monumental sculpture on the Coolsingel is by Naum Gabo. The external facing of the building is hexagonal travertine slabs; the great mass of the building rests on granite-faced columns at street level.

Below, UNESCO headquarters, Place de Fontenoy, Paris, designed in association with Bernard Zehrfuss and Pier Luigi Nervi. This air view of the model is from the south-east, and shows the façade of the Y-plan secretariat facing the Avenue de Saxe and the Avenue de Ségur; beyond is the conference building with its corrugated reinforced concrete end-walls and roof.

Victor Gruen

Victor Gruen, born in Vienna in 1903, is the son of a lawyer who died when Gruen was 15, leaving him with a warning not to become a lawyer, and a friend who was an architect and into whose office Gruen went after preliminary training. Parallel with his work in the office he studied at the Academy of Arts under Professor Behrens (passing an entrance examination which had been funked a few years earlier by Adolf Hitler). At the time, the strongest influences were Adolf Loos (whose obituary he wrote for a Viennese newspaper) and Le Corbusier, whose concepts of 'La Ville Radieuse' he wrote about in Austrian magazines. He spent nine years in the office of Melcher and Steiner, and then set up on his own, winning a prize in a housing competition entered with R. L. Baumfeld (one of his present partners in America) and Karl Langer (now practising in Australia). Since economic conditions didn't then favour large-scale building projects work in the office was mostly concerned with decoration and industrial design. A large commission for a department store coincided with the arrival of Hitler in Vienna; after three months, when all seemed lost, Gruen obtained a visa for the USA and in July 1938 left with his family, T-square, drawing board, books and $8. A period of struggle followed, during which Gruen helped to produce two shows on Broadway; then by chance he met a man he had known in Europe, who commissioned him to design a store.

The firm now has two production offices, in Los Angeles

Top left, the partnership, reading left to right, Contini, Baumfeld, Gruen, van Leuven.
Above right, Victor Gruen's first store-design in the USA, Lederer's Fifth Avenue, New York, completed just before World War II.
Right, ground level, and ramps to roof level, car park, of a department store outside Los Angeles, California, an early example of a new category of building developed since the war in the USA, the suburban shopping centre designed specifically for the motorist.